D1163530

Golf

Other titles in the Science Behind Sports series:

Golf

BY MICHAEL V. USCHAN

LUCENT BOOKS
A part of Gale, Cengage Learning

GALE
CENGAGE Learning·

Detroit • New York • San Francisco • New Haven, Conn • Waterville, Maine • London

I dedicate this book to Jerry Rogahn and Joe Totaraitis, two friends to "ride the golf carts with."

LIBRARY OF CONGRESS CATALOGING-IN-PUBLICATION DATA

Uschan, Michael V., 1948-
  Golf / by Michael V. Uschan.
    pages cm. -- (Science behind sports)
  Summary: "Lucent Books' "Science Behind Sports" Series explores the scientific principles behind some of the most popular team and individual sports, such as baseball, hockey, gymnastics, wrestling, swimming, and skiing. Each volume in the series focuses on one sport and opens with a brief look at the featured sport's origins, history and changes to rules, equipment, or techniques. Subsequent chapters cover the biomechanics and physiology of playing, related health and medical concerns, and the causes and treatment of sports-related injuries"-- Provided by publisher.
  Includes bibliographical references and index.
  ISBN 978-1-4205-1153-6 (hardback)
  1. Golf--Juvenile literature. 2. Sports sciences--Juvenile literatures. I. Greenhaven Press Editor. II. Title.
  GV965.U95 2013
  796.352--dc23
                                                           2013043173

Lucent Books
27500 Drake Rd
Farmington Hills MI 48331

ISBN-13: 978-1-4205-1153-6
ISBN-10: 1-4205-1153-X

TABLE OF CONTENTS

Foreword   6

Chapter 1
The History of Golf   8

Chapter 2
Golf and Physics   23

Chapter 3
Golf Biomechanics   38

Chapter 4
Training and Conditioning   52

Chapter 5
Golf Psychology   65

Chapter 6
Golf Technology   80

Notes   93
Glossary   97
For More Information   98
Index   100
Picture Credits   104
About the Author   104

On March 21, 1970, Slovenian ski jumper Vinko Bogataj took a terrible fall while competing at the Ski-flying World Championships in Oberstdorf, West Germany. Bogataj's pinwheeling crash was caught on tape by an ABC *Wide World of Sports* film crew and eventually became synonymous with "the agony of defeat" in competitive sporting. While many viewers were transfixed by the severity of Bogataj's accident, most were not aware of the biomechanical and environmental elements behind the skier's fall—heavy snow and wind conditions that made the ramp too fast and Bogataj's inability to maintain his center of gravity and slow himself down. Bogataj's accident illustrates that, no matter how mentally and physically prepared an athlete may be, scientific principles—such as momentum, gravity, friction, and aerodynamics—always have an impact on performance.

Lucent Book's Science Behind Sports series explores these and many more scientific principles behind some of the most popular team and individual sports, including baseball, hockey, gymnastics, wrestling, swimming, and skiing. Each volume in the series focuses on one sport or group of related sports. The volumes open with a brief look at the featured sport's origins, history and changes, then move on to cover the biomechanics and physiology of playing, related health and medical concerns, and the causes and treatment of sports-related injuries.

In addition to learning about the arc behind a curve ball, the impact of centripetal force on a figure skater, or how water buoyancy helps swimmers, Science Behind Sports readers will also learn how exercise, training, warming up, and diet and nutrition directly relate to peak performance and enjoyment of the sport. Volumes may also cover why certain sports are popular, how sports function in the business world, and which hot sporting issues—sports doping and cheating, for example—are in the news.

Basic physical science concepts, such as acceleration, kinetics, torque, and velocity, are explained in an engaging and accessible manner. The full-color text is augmented by fact boxes, sidebars, photos, and detailed diagrams, charts and graphs. In addition, a subject-specific glossary, bibliography and index provide further tools for researching the sports and concepts discussed throughout Science Behind Sports.

CHAPTER 1

The History of Golf

Many people consider St. Andrews Links golf course in St. Andrews, Scotland, to be the historic home of golf, because golfers have been playing there since the early 1400s. It is located on the shore of the North Sea, a site that is typical of the earliest golf courses. Centuries ago such sandy, seaside tracts of land were considered wasteland unsuitable for farming. They were used instead as open public spaces for leisure activities, such as picnicking, walking, and playing golf. Farmers also let their sheep graze on this land. By chomping on the grass and keeping it short, those hungry sheep actually made it easier for people to play golf.

In the twenty-first century, people still play golf at St. Andrews Links, but the game is nearly unrecognizable from the primitive one that golfers played in the 1400s. The first golfers played with clubs and balls made of wood. Modern-day golfers play with clubs and balls that are designed on computers and manufactured with space-age materials, incorporating scientific principles that make it easier for both professional and amateur golfers to hit better shots. Golfers today can ride motorized golf carts instead of walking 5 miles (8km) or more to play eighteen holes. They can also use electronic range finders to find exact distances to hit their shots to the the green, the end point of the hole. Thanks to American George Franklin Grant, inventor of the wooden golf tee, golfers no longer place their balls on small piles of sand before hitting them. And instead of wearing heavy pants and coats made of wool, a natural fabric, golfers today don garments manufactured from synthetic fabrics that keep them comfortable in the hottest or coldest weather and dry in the heaviest downpours.

Another significant change is the popularity of the game. Today golf is extremely popular around the world. Many people find it a fascinating, often addictive game. American Arnold Palmer, one of the greatest players in the history of professional golf, explains why millions of people love golf even though it is a very difficult game to play: "Golf is deceptively simple and endlessly complicated. A child can play it well and a grown man can never master it. [It] is almost a science, yet it is a puzzle without an answer. [It] satisfies the soul and frustrates the intellect. It is at the same time rewarding and maddening—and it is without doubt the greatest game mankind has ever invented."[1]

The Origin of Golf

No one knows who actually invented golf or when. One theory is that Scottish shepherds were the first golfers. Bored with watching their wooly charges graze along seaside stands of tall grass, the shepherds began striking small rocks with the curved part of the wooden staffs they used to herd their sheep. When a rock accidentally fell into a hole, they tried to repeat that success, and golf was born.

Striking a ball-like object to see how far or how accurately one can hit it is common in many different types of sports throughout history in every part of the world. The Romans as early as the first century played *paganica*, a game in which players used bent sticks to hit a leather ball stuffed with feathers or wool. *Dakyu* is an ancient Japanese game from the eighth century in which players, either on foot or riding horses, used sticks to hit balls into a hoop on the ground. During the twelfth century, Belgians played a game called *chole*, in which players wielded iron clubs to

A portion of a scroll created in China around the fourteenth century shows members of the imperial court playing a golf-like game called suigan.

hit egg-shaped wooden balls, with some blows propelling the ball up to 400 yards (366m). Illustrated Chinese scrolls from the fourteenth century show images of *suigan*, a game in which people struck a ball with a stick while walking. *Jeu de mail*, a French game from the fifteenth century, was a similar game in which players used long-handled mallets to smack wooden balls. According to golf historians, the stick-and-ball game that most closely resembles golf is *kolven*, a game that originated in the Netherlands in the 1200s. This sport was also known in Dutch as *kolf* or *colf*, terms that are nearly identical to the word *golf*, even though it was far different from the sport known today by that name. Played both indoors and outdoors, sometimes even on ice, *kolven*

Benjamin Rush

Benjamin Rush (1745–1813) was an American doctor, teacher, author, and patriot. He was also one of the signers of the Declaration of Independence. In his book, *Sermons to Gentleman upon Temperance and Exercise*, Rush praises golf as a way to stay physically fit. He writes,

> Golf is an exercise which is much used by the Gentlemen in Scotland. A large common, in which there are several little holes, is chosen for the purpose. It is played with little leather balls stuffed with feathers, and sticks made somewhat in the form of a handy-wicket [wooden club]. He who puts a ball into a given number of holes with the fewest strokes, gets [wins] the game. A man would live ten years the longer for using this exercise once or twice a week.

Quoted in Lawrence Sheehan. *A Passion for Golf: Treasures and Traditions of the Game*. New York: Clarkson Potter, 1994, p. 86.

involved using large clubs to smash large, heavy balls that weighed several pounds. The outdoor game involved hitting the balls through doors of homes and other structures, while the indoor version had players strike the ball into marked areas. In both versions members of an opposing team would attempt to stop players from advancing the ball.

Kolven may have influenced the development of the game that originated in Scotland and eventually came to be known as golf. In his book, *The Story of Golf*, golf historian George Peper notes that Scotland and the Netherlands, separated only by a relatively short expanse of sea, have been trading partners for many centuries. The theory is that in addition to trading goods, the two countries exchanged bits of each other's cultures, including their sporting activities. However, Peper and many other sports historians argue that golf is a separate and unique sport from *kolven* and that it was born in Scotland. He writes, "But, no matter where the seeds of golf were sown, without question it was the Scots [the people of Scotland] who gave the game its unique character, the Scots who combined the elements of distance off the tee and deftness into the green, and the Scots who ingrained the notion of each player advancing independently toward the hole, without interference from his opponents."[2]

Golf History

The first written reference to golf is a proclamation by King James II of Scotland on March 6, 1457. It states "that futeball [soccer] and golfe be cryed down [prohibited] and not used."[3] The king banned these activities because his nation was at war with England at the time, and he feared his soldiers would play the popular sports instead of practicing their archery. Scottish officials attempted to ban golf again in 1471 and 1491, but enough players ignored the decrees to keep the sport alive until 1502, when Scotland and England signed a peace treaty. By 1559 even Scottish royalty was playing golf, including Queen Mary (commonly known as Mary, Queen of Scots), one of the first female golfers. In 1603 King James VI of Scotland, Mary's son, also became the king of England (making him James I of Great Britain), and he took the game with him to England.

Most of the first courses, like those at St. Andrews Links, were links courses, built along the shores of seas; the term *links course* refers specifically to a seaside course. The name for this type of course comes from the Scottish word *hlinc*, meaning rising ground or ridge, which aptly describes the contours of the gently curving sand dunes bordering the shoreline. Such lands were ready-made for golf. Courses that came later, especially those in the United States, are called parkland courses, because they are inland from the sea. Parkland courses are routed through stands of trees, and most also have ponds or rivers.

Having bodies of water on a course is deliberate, because they make the courses more challenging. In addition to trees and water, players also have to contend with sand traps and high grass called rough. The object of golf is to hit the ball into holes in as few strokes as possible, and to do that players

have to strategically plan their shots to avoid such hazards. In his book, *Grounds for Golf*, Geoff Shackleford, an expert in golf course design, writes, "If the architect has done his job, the avenue to the hole that leads to a lower scoring possibility should be more dangerous than the longer, safer route."[4] All modern golf courses have some hazards, but many courses are designed to keep hazards at a minimum, so that golfers can enjoy playing while still testing their skills.

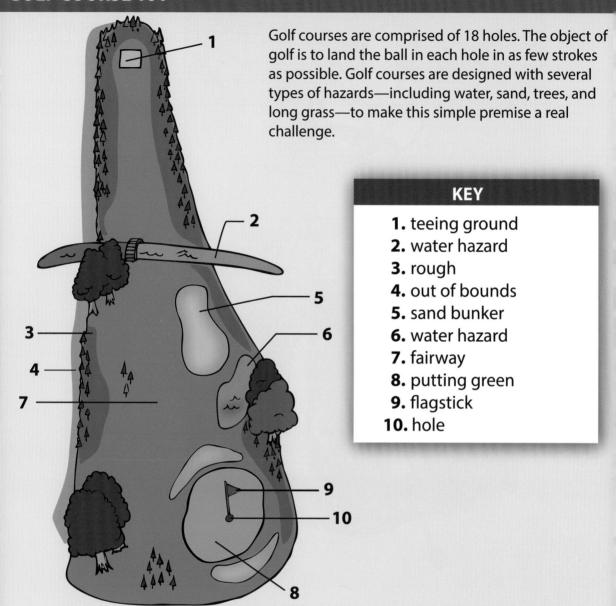

Golf courses are comprised of 18 holes. The object of golf is to land the ball in each hole in as few strokes as possible. Golf courses are designed with several types of hazards—including water, sand, trees, and long grass—to make this simple premise a real challenge.

KEY

1. teeing ground
2. water hazard
3. rough
4. out of bounds
5. sand bunker
6. water hazard
7. fairway
8. putting green
9. flagstick
10. hole

Despite the primitive wooden balls and clubs early golfers wielded, they played golf much the same way as people do today. They hit their first shots from a tee area into the fairway, an expanse of short grass that winds its way to a green, which is the area where each hole is located. Once their ball was on the green, golfers putted (hit) it into a small hole in the ground. In the early years of golf, people played informally. Individual golfers or groups of players determined the rules, how many yards (meters) long the holes should be, equipment standards, and other factors; there was no standardization of the sport. This began to change when devotees of the sport banded together to form clubs and began making golf a more formal, organized activity.

Golf Rules Evolve

In 1744 a group of men who played golf together in Scotland founded the first golf club, the Gentlemen Golfers of Leith (later renamed the Honourable Company of

A group of golfers play a round at the Royal and Ancient Golf Club of St. Andrews, Scotland's most famous course, in 1798.

Golf Glossary

birdie: A score one stroke less than par.

bogey: A score one stroke over par.

double eagle: A score three strokes less than par.

drive (or tee shot): The golfer's first shot on each hole.

eagle: A score two strokes less than par.

fairway: The short grass area that is the intended route from the tee to the green.

flagstick: A pole with an attached flag to show golfers where the hole is.

fringe: Short but slightly longer grass bordering the green.

green: Extremely short-cut grass on which players putt the ball into the hole.

hole (or cup): A cavity, 4.25 inches (10.80cm) wide and 4 inches (10.16cm) deep, cut out of the green.

hole in one (or ace): A tee shot that finishes in the cup.

rough: Longer grass bordering the fairway and surrounding the green.

par: The score a good player should make on a hole or the total number of strokes to play nine or eighteen holes.

tee (tee box): The area in which golfers must stand to hit their first shots on each hole.

Edinburgh Golfers). On April 2, 1744, eleven members of the club played their first championship on the Links of Leith, a course with only five holes. Physician John Rattray won that first recorded golf competition and received a silver golf club as a prize. That same year, club members approved the first thirteen rules of golf. Some are still in effect today, including the rule that says which player goes first after golfers hit their tee shots: "He whose ball lyest farthest from the hole is obliged to play first."[5] In 1768 the Gentlemen Golfers of Leith also built the first golf clubhouse, the building in which golfers can change clothes and gather socially before or after golfing.

Scotland's most famous golf club is the Royal and Ancient Golf Club of St. Andrews (R&A), which twenty-two golfers started in 1754. A written account of the club's history provides an explanation for its founding: "The Noblemen and Gentlemen [being] admired of the Ancient and healthful exercise of the Golf, and at the same time having the interest and prosperity of the ancient city of St Andrews at heart, being the Alma Mater of the Golf."[6]

In the late eighteenth century golf was played only in Scotland and England. The R&A quickly became the preeminent club in the sport because of innovations its members made that improved the game. For example, in 1764 it decided to reduce the number of holes at one of the courses at St. Andrews Links golf course from twenty-two to eighteen. Other golf courses, which had courses with varying numbers of holes, quickly adopted eighteen holes as the standard. In 1897 the R&A standardized all the rules of golf. R&A's prestige was so great that it became the sole body responsible for making and updating the game's rules. In 1952, however, the R&A began cooperating with the United States Golf Association (USGA), founded in 1894 as the Amateur Golf Association of the United States, to jointly authorize the rules that govern golf globally.

Over several centuries, rules and traditions developed in Scotland, England, and the United States have shaped the way people play golf. Holes of different lengths were assigned a standard value of par, the number of strokes a good golfer should need to hit the ball into each hole. The rules of golf also limit the length of holes according to par—a par three can be no longer than 250 yards (229m); a par four must be between 251 yards (230m) and 470 yards (430m); and a par five is 471 yards (431m) or longer. However, in some professional events holes as long as 500 yards (457m) are played as a par four so that they will be more challenging for the longer-hitting professional players. And some par five holes can be 600 yards (549m) or even longer. One rule even

African Americans and Golf

In the United States African Americans were not allowed to compete in amateur golf events until the 1950s, and they were barred from Professional Golf Association (PGA) tournaments until 1961. In 1967 African American Charlie Sifford won the Greater Hartford Open Invitational and became the first black champion on the Professional Golf Association (PGA) of America Tour. Today African American Tiger Woods is considered by many to be the greatest golfer in the sport's history. As of the 2013 season, Woods had won seventy-nine PGA Tour events, including fourteen majors (the four major championships in professional golf are the Masters, U.S. Open, British Open, and PGA Championship). He was second in PGA career wins to Sam Snead, who had eighty-two, and second in major victories to Jack Nicklaus, who has eighteen. Many observers believe Woods will eventually surpass both Snead, who died in 2002 at the age of eighty-nine, and Nicklaus, who

retired in 2005. Woods is also the only golfer to win all four professional majors consecutively. After winning his first major in 1997, Woods hugged Sifford, who was watching, and said, "Thanks for making this possible."

Quoted in Rick Reilly. "Strokes of Genius." *Sports Illustrated*, April 21, 1997. http://sportsillustrated.cnn.com/vault/article/magazine/MAG1009901/index.htm.

In 1967 Charlie Sifford, seen here in 1969, became the first African American to win a championship on the PGA tour.

regulates the size of the hole golfers putt into after reaching the green: It must be 4.25 inches (10.80cm) in diameter and 4 inches (10.16cm) deep.

The rules that govern golf are still evolving and changing, even in the twenty-first century. On November 28, 2012, the R&A and USGA banned long putters, a type of club that golfers anchor against their chest or stomach to make it easier to hit putts straight. USGA executive director Mike Davis explains why the USGA prohibited long putters: "The player's challenge is to control the movement of the entire club in striking the ball, and anchoring the club [against the chest or stomach] alters the nature of that challenge."[7] The ban, however, applies only to golfers participating in formal amateur or professional competitions. The new rule does not take effect until 2016 so that golfers currently using long putters will have time to adjust without damaging their ability to play.

The Growth of Golf

In the nineteenth century Great Britain began expanding its economic and political control in other parts of the world, including Africa, India, and Asia, and British merchants and soldiers helped spread golf to new countries by building courses

John Reid, right, joins other golfers for a round at St. Andrew's Golf Club in Yonkers, New York, in 1888.

HOLE IN ONE

Golf was so unknown in the United States in 1887 that a policeman almost arrested Robert Lockhart for hitting some shots in Central Park in New York City. The policeman left Lockhart alone after realizing he had not broken any laws even though what he was doing looked strange.

and playing golf. In 1829 the Royal Calcutta Golf Club in India became the first golf course outside Great Britain. It was followed by Royal Adelaide in Australia in 1871, Royal Cape in South Africa in 1885, Royal Hong Kong in 1889, Royal Bangkok in Thailand in 1890, Shanghai Golf Club in China in 1896, and Kobe Golf Club in Kobe, Japan, in 1903.

Historians estimate that golf appeared in what is now the United States sometime in the 1700s. Evidence that the colonists (known later as Americans) played golf include a 1779 newspaper from the colony of New York that published an advertisement for golf balls and a 1788 newspaper from the state of South Carolina that ran a story about a social function at the South Carolina Golf Club. Although there is no historical evidence that anyone during the 1700s played regularly on a proper golf course, the newspapers suggest that Americans probably played golf informally.

The first golf game for which written records exist occurred on January 22, 1888. On that date John Reid, a Scotsman, played with several friends on a makeshift course in a cow pasture near his home in Yonkers, New York. The men enjoyed playing so much that they moved to a larger pasture and created a six-hole course. After winter ended their playing season on November 14, they established the St. Andrew's Golf Club. Reid later became known as the father of American golf, and as of the year 2013, St. Andrew's Golf Club still exists and holds the distinction of being the oldest, continuously existing golf club in the United States.

Golf in the United States grew with lightning speed in the late nineteenth century. More than one thousand courses were built in the 1890s, including Chicago Golf Club in Wheaton, Illinois. It was the first to have eighteen holes. While most golf courses in Great Britain are links layouts, U.S. courses were built inland and are parkland courses. The American courses feature well-kept greens and fairways,

rough, sand traps, and dangerous bodies of water. They often have dramatic elevation changes, featuring tee areas perched high above the fairway. The Chicago Golf Club and most early courses were built at existing private clubs in which wealthy members already swam, played tennis, rode horses, and played polo.

Francis Ouimet inspired many ordinary Americans to take up the sport of golf after his victory at the U.S. Open championship in 1913.

Golf for Everyone

When golf began in Scotland centuries ago, the sport was open to everyone. Peper writes, "The greatest and wisest of the land were to be seen mingling freely with the humblest mechanics in the pursuit of their common and beloved amusement. All distinctions of rank were leveled by the joyous spirit of the game."[8]

Over time, however, golf became too expensive for most people, because of fees they had to pay to join private clubs. Golf thus became a sport only for the rich. In addition, women golfers and members of minority groups were often not welcome, with many private clubs not allowing them to join or play their courses. This was true around the world, including in the United States. However, in the twentieth century, when women and African Americans began to gain equal rights, most private clubs slowly began to accept them. Even in the twenty-first century, a few private clubs still restrict their membership on the basis of race and gender, even though they are more accessible to people from all economic levels.

In 1913 American amateur golfer Francis Ouimet defeated two of the game's top professional players, Britain's Harry Vardon and Ted Ray, in an eighteen-hole play-off to win the U.S. Open championship at the Country Club in Brookline, Massachusetts. His victory was a turning point in golf, because he was an amateur and because he came from a working-class family. Ouimet had even worked as a caddy (a person who carries a golfer's clubs during a game) at the Country Club, which his family was too poor to join. According to golf historian Herbert Warren Wind, the victory made Ouimet an American hero and changed the perception of the sport in the United States. In his book, *The Story of American Golf*, Wind writes, "Overnight the non-wealthy American lost his antagonism toward golf. He had been wrong, he felt, in tagging it a society sport. After all, the Open Champion was a fine, clean-cut American boy from the same walk of life as himself."[9]

Ouimet's victory inspired hundreds of thousands of average people to start playing golf and ignited a building boom of public golf courses that gave them access to the game. By the 1920s there were 2 million American golfers and by 1950 that number had doubled to 4 million. Thanks in large part to the elimination of almost all racial and gender discrimination that kept women and minorities from playing golf, the number of U.S. golfers exploded to 29 million by 2012 according to the National Golf Foundation. The United States has more golfers than any other nation.

CHAPTER **2**

Golf and Physics

On April 8, 2012, Bubba Watson, an American professional golfer, hit a remarkable shot to win the
Masters Tournament, one of golf's four major championships, held at Augusta National Golf Club in Augusta,
Georgia. (The four main championships in professional
golf—known as the majors—are the Masters, U.S. Open,
British Open, and PGA Championship.) The shot curved
wildly out of an opening in a stand of trees and somehow
made its way to the green. Watson was competing against
South African Louis Oosthuizen in a play-off, after they had
tied with scores of ten-under par after seventy-two holes.
They had both parred the first play-off hole, the eighteenth.
But on the second play-off hole Watson hit a terrible tee
shot, and his ball landed in trees bordering the right side of
the fairway. The play-off was sudden death, which means
that the first golfer to win a hole would win the tournament.
Watson was in trouble, because he could not see the green
from where he stood over his ball. There was a gap in the
trees through which he could hit his ball, but the green was
at almost a right angle from the relatively straight shot he
needed to escape the trees. To get his ball on the green, Watson would have to intentionally hit a low, sweeping shot,
known as a hook, that would start straight out of the trees
and then drastically cut to the right toward the green.

Watson is a confident, creative golfer, who enjoys the challenge of hitting difficult shots. The first time Watson met his

caddy, Ted Scott, he said, "If I have a swing, I've got a shot,"[10] which means that if he has the opportunity to swing, then he has a chance to be successful, no matter how difficult the shot might appear. So that day at the 2012 Masters Tournament, Watson decided to try the difficult shot from the trees despite the pressure. His shot was amazing. The ball flew straight out of the trees and then curved in a wide arc to the green, where it came to rest 10 feet (3m) from the hole. Watson then hit two putts to make par four and win the hole and the championship. Later, Watson described his amazing shot: "I think we had like 164 yards to the hole, give or take, in that area, maybe a little less. And I hit my 52-degree, my [wedge], hooked it about 40 yards, hit it about 15 feet off the ground until it got under the tree, and then it started rising—pretty easy."[11]

Thousands of spectators lining the hole, as well as tens of millions of people around the world watching on television, were stunned by his miraculous shot. It became one of the most celebrated shots in major golf tournament history. Watson knew how to physically hit that winning shot. What is unknown is whether Watson knew the scientific principles that dictated how his ball would react when he struck it the way he did. For that, he would have had to know physics, an important and complex science that can be used to understand why Watson's shot flew the way it did.

Physics and Golf

The word *physics* comes from *physikos*, a Greek word for natural sciences. Physics is the science that concerns matter and energy, including the behavior of physical objects when they meet various forces. Physicists John McLester and Peter St. Pierre have studied how the laws of physics dictate what happens to a golf ball when it is struck by a golf club. They say that golfers who want to understand the science of their sport must study Newton's laws of motion, the basic physics principles that English physicist and mathematician Sir Isaac

Newton discovered in the seventeenth century. In their book, *Applied Biomechanics: Concepts and Connections*, McLester and St. Pierre write,

> From the initial contact with the club at impact, the golf ball is subject only to the laws of physics. Newton's Laws of Motion can be used to calculate every detail about the golf ball in motion whether in the air or rolling along a putting green. Golf balls in flight can gain altitude against gravity, turn right and left, fly high or low [because] Newtonian laws of motion govern all of these situations.[12]

In his groundbreaking 1687 work, *Philosophiae Naturalis Principia Mathematica* (*Mathematical Principles of Natural Philosophy*), Newton formulates three laws of motion that are still relevant in the twenty-first century in studying the motion of objects. They can be summarized as:

A club striking a golf ball illustrates Newton's laws of motion, as the movement of the ball is subject to the force of the club.

I. Every object in a state of uniform motion tends to remain in that state of motion unless an external force is applied to it.

II. The relationship between an object's mass m, its acceleration a, and the applied force F is $F = ma$. Acceleration and force are vectors [individual elements that can move and exert force]; in this law the direction of the force vector is the same as the direction of the acceleration vector [which means that the force applied in one direction sends the object traveling in that same direction].

III. For every action there is an equal and opposite reaction.[13]

Newton's first law as applied to golf is easily understood: A golf ball remains where it is until the force of a club hitting it moves it. The second law concerns how fast the ball will move (its acceleration) when struck by the club, with the ball moving in the same direction as the club. The third law means that every time a club strikes a ball, the force of the meeting affects them both.

Newton also discovered gravity, the natural phenomenon that continually exerts its own force to pull objects to the ground. It is also important in understanding the physical principles that explain how a ball reacts when a golfer strikes it with a club.

Gravity and Newton's laws of motion affect a golf ball at different times and in various ways during the swing as well as the ball's trajectory to its target after it has been struck. It is important to consider them all when trying to understand the science that determines how far and in which direction golf shots will go.

The Swing

Theodore P. Jorgensen was an American physicist who helped develop the atomic bomb during World War II (1939–1945). He was also an avid golfer who wrote the book, *The Physics of Golf*. In his book Jorgensen focuses on the golf swing, which he claims is a "dynamic process" ruled by Newton's laws of motion. He writes, "The stroke may be considered as a consequence of three separate events: the swing of the club, the impact of the clubhead with the ball, and the flight of the ball toward the target."[14]

The swing is the moving element in the collision that occurs between a golf club and golf ball. Golfers who drive the ball 300 yards (274m) have efficient, powerful swings that allow them to swing at speeds of more than 100 miles per hour (161kmh). Golfers use a variety of muscles in their body during the swing to generate that speed and power, including those in their arms, shoulders, legs, buttocks, back, and abdomen. In his book, *Newton on the Tee*, science writer John Zumerchik claims that "swing power is, in essence, fined-tuned control of explosiveness [explosive power]."[15]

Molecular Golf

The collision between a golf ball and a golf club initially takes place at the molecular level. In their book, *Applied Biomechanics: Concepts and Connections*, John McLester and Peter St. Pierre explain that when impact occurs, it causes a molecular change that momentarily changes the shape of the ball:

> Slow motion pictures of golf balls, baseballs, and other objects being hit with blunt force show them going out of shape for a fraction of a second on impact. They naturally return to their original form. [The] force imparted by the golf club creates changes in motion within the molecular structure of the ball and causes certain areas of the ball to move from their original position. After leaving the clubface, those molecules return to their original positions relative to the others because of the elastic properties of the material—a stored force within the ball that creates motion and returns the ball to its original shape.

John McLester and Peter St. Pierre. *Applied Biomechanics: Concepts and Connections*. Belmont, CA: Wadsworth, 2007, p. 360.

The shape of the ball is momentarily changed when it is struck by the force of the club.

THE POWER BEHIND THE SWING

Golfers use many muscles during a swing to generate the speed and power to hit the ball. This illustration shows some of the muscles used during the backswing portion of the golf swing.

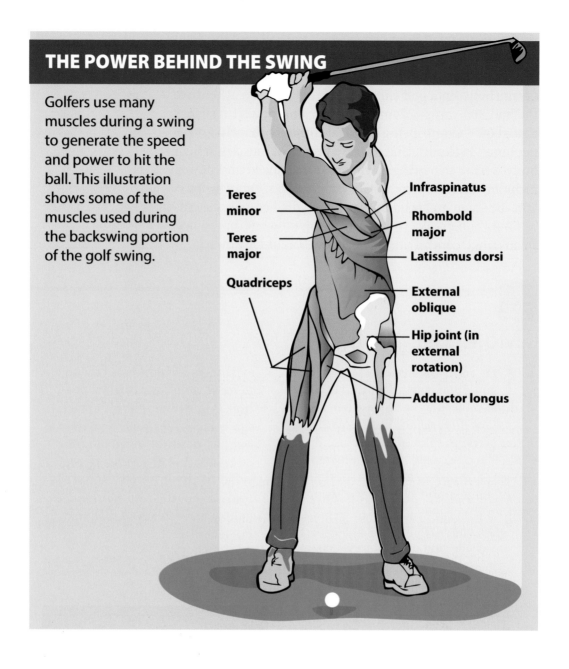

Teres minor

Teres major

Quadriceps

Infraspinatus

Rhombold major

Latissimus dorsi

External oblique

Hip joint (in external rotation)

Adductor longus

This explosiveness is the force the clubhead transmits to the ball, which results in a transfer of energy that moves the ball out of a state of inertia (nonmovement) to one of acceleration (movement). This is where Newton's second law of motion applies. The explosive impact that occurs when the clubhead meets the ball can be described by this simple mathematical equation: Force = mass x acceleration. Mathematicians use this basic formula to determine how much force is applied in an impact and how the velocities (speeds) of the two colliding objects change.

The actual collision between a clubhead and a ball lasts just 0.0005 seconds. Despite being such a small amount of time, that fraction of a second is the most important moment in any golf swing. Golfers often swing as fast as possible on many of their shots, especially their opening shot on each hole, because the speed of the clubhead when it strikes the ball is the most important factor in generating the power that golfers need to hit balls a long way. For example, someone who

Ground Transfer

Although most golfers do not know it, the ground they play golf on is a source of power to their swing. In their book, *Golf Anatomy*, Craig Davies and Vince DiSaia explain that golfers generate some of the power in their swing through the physics reaction that occurs between their body and the ground. They write,

> For maximal power creation with minimal negative stress on the body, the ground must be the first link in the chain of energy transfer. Newton's third law of motion states that for every force applied by one object into a second, an equal and opposite force is applied from the second object back to the first. As such, using the legs to drive forcefully into the ground [during the swing] results in the ground pushing back up into the golfer's body with an equal magnitude force. The force the ground transmits into the golfer is known is as the ground reaction force (GRF). GRF is then transferred through the legs and into the pelvis. From the pelvis the force is transferred into the golfer's core, shoulder complex, arms, and, finally, the golf club and ball.

Craig Davies and Vince DiSaia. *Golf Anatomy*. Champaign, IL: Human Kinetics, 2010, p. 4.

hits a ball with a swing speed of 80 miles per hour (129kmh) will drive it about 180 yards (165m), while a swing speed of 105 miles per hour (169kmh) produces a drive of 260 yards (238m) or longer. Long tee shots, for example, make it easier for golfers to score well on any hole. Hitting a long first shot on short, par-three holes gives golfers a chance to reach the green in one stroke, while long-distance drives on longer holes reduces the distance they have to reach the green on succeeding shots.

Distance, however, is not the only important result of a shot. Hitting the ball straight is sometimes more important. Balls that do not fly straight can land in the rough, trees, or sand traps and make a golfer's next shot difficult. When the ball lands in water, the next shot is impossible. The key to hitting straight shots is to have the face of the club meet the ball squarely. When that does not happen, the shot flies out of line from the intended target, because the ball is obeying the laws of physics.

Aerodynamics

Any object that flies through the air is considered a projectile, and its path is called a trajectory. Many factors influence the trajectory of a projectile, whether it is a football thrown by a quarterback, a golf ball struck by a golfer, or a bullet fired out of a gun. The study of the forces that affect objects as they pass through the air, which include the downward pull of gravity and the resistance of air that flows around the object, is known as aerodynamics. There are two distinct forces in aerodynamics: lift and drag. Lift is divided between positive and negative effects on the ball because of how much and in which direction the ball spins. Drag is a negative force that works to impede how far a golf ball travels.

When the clubhead meets the ball, the ball slides slightly up the clubhead because of its loft, the angle at which the face of the club is attached to the shaft of the club. The blow of the club produces backspin. This backward revolution of the ball on a horizontal axis combines with the forward velocity of the swing to produce an upward force stronger than the downward force that gravity exerts

on everything. Thus, it is this spin that enables the ball to rise into the air. A golf ball's spin rate refers to the speed that it spins on its axis while in flight, and it is measured in revolutions per minute (rpm). A ball hit by an average male golfer will have an rpm of twenty-eight hundred to thirty-five hundred, and a ball hit by an average female golfer will have an rpm of three thousand to four thousand. The amount of spin produced depends on several factors, including the club's loft and the speed of the club at impact with the ball. Spin produces lift, which helps

Colorized two-dimensional fluid flow surrounding a moving golf ball shows the ball's backspin, which creates lift, an upward force that causes the ball to rise in the air.

Golf Balls Spin

In the late 1800s Peter Guthrie Tait (1831–1901), a Scottish physicist and mathematician, conducted studies on the flight of golf balls. He was the first person to prove that golf balls spin when struck. Tait did this by fastening one end of a long piece of tape to a golf ball and the other end to the ground and then striking the ball with a golf club. When Tait unraveled the tape, he discovered it had been twisted at the rate of 40 to 120 times per second. There were no high-speed cameras or other devices in Tait's lifetime that could prove golf balls spun, but the tape, a primitive test device, proved for the first time that golf balls spin.

the ball become airborne and travel farther; thus higher spin rates produce longer shots. However, spin can also adversely affect shots.

Spin's negative nature appears when the clubhead does not meet the ball squarely, which occurs when the club strikes the ball from an angle rather than straight on. Such swings are known as mishits and cause sidespin in which balls spin either clockwise or counterclockwise around their vertical axis. Australian professional golfer Greg Norman, the top-ranked golfer in the world for several years in the late 1980s and early 1990s, explains how sidespin affects shots: "When you cut across the ball, either from out to in or from in to out, you impart sidespin along with the backspin. It is this sidespin that causes the ball to curve to the right or left."[16]

When a ball spins left to right, its trajectory heads to the right in either a fade or slice, and when a ball spins right to left, it goes left in either a draw or a hook. Fade and draw are terms that refer to balls that curve left or right only slightly from the trajectory a straight shot would take; many players try to produce such shots to position their balls on fairways or greens. Slices and hooks, however, curve more severely than fades or draws from a path straight down the fairway; they are mistakes that result in terrible shots. Although professional golfers like Watson can deliberately make their balls curve one way or the other to achieve a trajectory that will help them, average golfers often hit such shots accidentally, and it can hurt their game.

Drag is a negative force on balls, which means that it limits how far balls can travel. One of the most powerful elements creating drag is the composition of the atmosphere. The power the atmosphere exerts on the ball is dependent on its three natural conditions: pressure, temperature, and humidity. Higher atmospheric pressure, colder tempera-tures, and higher humidity all make it harder for balls to fly through the air because they create resistance and limit how far the balls can travel.

The opposite atmospheric conditions lessen drag's effects on balls. For example, playing at a higher altitude provides shots with a power boost, because air pressure is lower at higher elevations. An accepted rule of thumb for golfers is that their shots will travel 10 percent farther for every 5,000 feet (1,524m) they are above sea level. Thus, the same shot that travels 150 yards (137m) at sea level will fly 165 yards (151m) at 5,000 feet (1,524m). Warmer weather and drier conditions also reduce drag on shots and allow balls to fly farther. Wind is another factor that can dramatically affect ball flight. Its effects, too, can be either good or bad. Wind shortens or lengthens shots, depending on which way it is blowing, and can send balls right or left of the golfer's target. When golfers suffer mishits for any reason, their shots can wind up in hazards and that means trouble for even the best professionals.

Shots from Hazards

The hazard many golfers dread the most is the sand trap, which is also called a bunker. Traps can be huge or small and shallow or deep, and they come in almost any shape. The number of sand traps on courses can also vary widely. There are 112 sand traps on the Old Course at St. Andrews Links in Scotland, but more than 900 at Whistling Straits at the American Club in Wisconsin in the United States.

HITTING OUT OF A SAND TRAP

Shots from sand traps require a completely different swing than those made on grass. To successfully hit out of sand, a golfer should know two things: First, instead of hitting the ball directly, a golfer must hit the sand behind and beneath the ball in order to lift the ball out of the sand. Second, a stroke of greater force is needed because the sand between the golf club head and ball absorbs some of the energy of the stroke; thus, without a more forceful hit it is unlikely the ball will clear the sand trap.

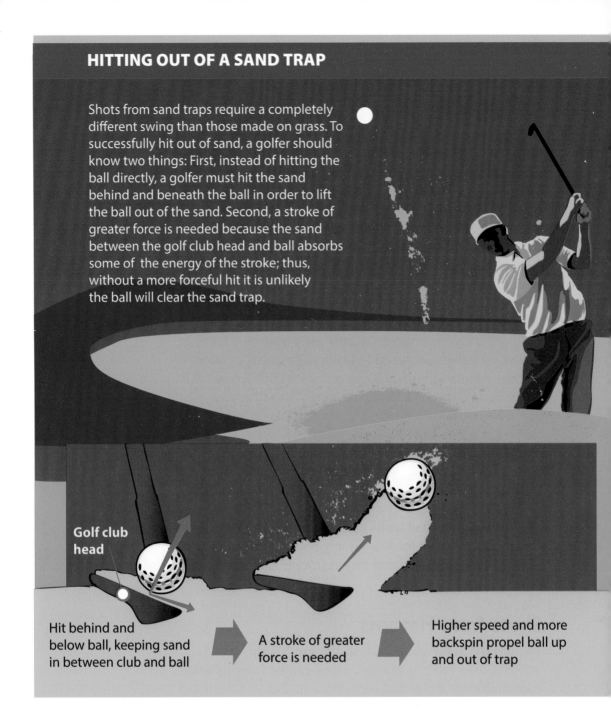

Golf club head

Hit behind and below ball, keeping sand in between club and ball

A stroke of greater force is needed

Higher speed and more backspin propel ball up and out of trap

Hitting a ball that is sitting in a sand trap is difficult because it requires a completely different swing than the one needed to hit balls off grass. Instead of directly striking their balls, golfers must hit behind them with their club heads to propel them out of the sand trap. Norman explains, "Sand play is elementary physics. I was never a science whiz in school, but I learned enough to know that if you push the sand in the correct manner, it will transfer your energy and lift the ball in the way you want it to fly. It's basic earthmoving."[17]

The problem with hitting a ball out of a sand trap is that the sand between the club and ball absorbs some of the energy of the stroke. Thus golfers have to swing harder to hit balls the same distance out of sand than they do on grass, and that makes it difficult for them to judge how hard to hit sand shots. Golfers also have to struggle with how far behind the ball their club should enter the sand, something that also affects distance. Strokes farther behind the ball force the golfer to expend more energy in the stroke by having to move more sand, thus limiting how far the ball will travel.

Shots out of the rough that borders greens and fairways are also harder than those on the fairway. The grass on the fairway is cut short, but in the rough, long blades of grass can get between the ball and the club. When that happens, the laws of physics can again produce a bad shot. The lack of solid contact between the club and the ball can produce backspin, which makes the ball fly higher and farther—hence the name "flier" for such shots—and those often travel beyond the intended target. A lack of backspin also means that balls roll farther when they strike the ground, which can also send them past the target area.

Because of these complications, golfers often hit fliers out of the rough. Since the goal of such shots is to get as close to the hole as possible so golfers can finish the hole in as few putts as possible, this can be disastrous.

Putting

Shots in golf can be more than 300 yards (274m) or only 2 inches (5.1cm). Yet they all count the same when golfers add up their score. Putting is when golfers use a special club called a putter to tap their balls for short distances on greens until they get them in the hole. Newton's laws of motion regarding velocity and the direction a ball takes when struck

Striking the ball squarely with the face of the putter is key to making a straight putt. Friction and force are also factors that affect the trajectory of a putt.

also apply to balls hit with putters, even though the balls travel on grass instead of through the air.

The holes on golf courses are only 4.25 inches (10.80cm) in diameter—a small target that can be easy to miss. As in strokes with other clubs, the key to hitting a straight putt is to have the face of the putter contact the ball squarely. Having the putter head strike the ball at any angle but straight on creates sidespin that sends the ball rolling off the intended direction. It is the same reaction as a mishit for a ball struck through the air. In his book, *The Science of Golf*, John Wesson writes, "An error in the alignment of the face of the putter is [serious]. An error angle of 1 percent for the face of the putter would mean that the ball would miss the hole in a 13-foot putt."[18]

Another important element in successful putting is determining how hard to hit the ball. What makes this task difficult is friction between the ball and the surface it rolls over. Zumerchik writes, "Friction impedes the progress of any object, but is also the reason a ball rolls; without it, a ball would slide like a hockey puck. Friction creates a braking force at the point the ball meets the surface."[19] Determining how hard to hit the ball to overcome friction is vitally important; a putt hit too softly will stop short of the hole and one hit too hard may go so far past the hole that the golfer will have trouble making the next putt.

Putting has many other variables, including strong winds and debris on the green, that can send balls off the intended direction as they approach the hole. There are so many factors involved in hitting a good putt that putting is one of the most difficult parts of golf. But Zumerchik, a former editor of American Institute of Physics publications, believes that knowledge of the science underlying golf can help golfers, even with these variable challenges. In *Newton on the Tee: A Good Walk Through the Science of Golf*, Zumerchik writes, "The dynamics involved in golf are indeed complex, which is why an understanding of the underlying science can serve you well. It won't guarantee answers, but it certainly can give you the wisdom to ask the right questions [to improve play]."[20]

CHAPTER 3

Golf Biomechanics

During a game of golf, players hit their ball in a number of different ways. They will usually swing as hard as they can on their opening drive to produce a long, soaring shot that travels 300 yards (274m) or more. Golfers then use different types of clubs to hit shorter and shorter shots until their ball reaches the green. Generating power is an important factor in hitting many shots, but once their ball reaches the green, golfers wield a putter to hit it just a few yards or even inches, until it reaches the hole. Sometimes the ball will seem to defy gravity and stop on the very edge of the hole without dropping in. But whether it is a lengthy drive or a putt that knocks a ball sitting on the edge of the hole into the hole, each stroke counts the same on the golfer's scorecard.

In order to perform all of the different shots necessary in golf, players must use a wide variety of muscles and body motions. The branch of science that studies the forces that produce motion and the effects of motion on objects is called mechanics, and biomechanics is the use of mechanics to study athletic performance. In an article for the journal *Sports Medicine*, Patria A. Hume, Justin Keogh, and Duncan Reid describe how the study of biomechanics can be applied to golf. They write, "Golf biomechanics applies the principles and technique of mechanics to the structure and function of the golfer in an effort to improve golf technique and performance. Therefore, a biomechanical assessment of the golf

Using Biomechanics in Golf

Scientists who study biomechanics in golf have a simple goal: to help golfers improve their play. In an article in the journal *Sports Medicine*, Patria A. Hume, Justin Keogh, and Duncan Reid write,

> By using qualitative and quantitative biomechanical analyses tools, biomechanists have been able to describe the movement patterns of golfer's swings as well as the resultant joint torques and patterns of muscle activity that produce these movements. Biomechanics has been used in an attempt to characterize the "ideal" golf swing, with the aim of improving performance and reducing the risk and severity of golf-related injuries. Biomechanical studies have assessed the kinematic, kinetic and [other physical] characteristics of the golf swing.

Patria A. Hume, Justin Keogh, and Duncan Reid. "The Role of Biomechanics in Maximising Distance and Accuracy of Golf Shots." *Sports Medicine* 35, no. 5 (2005): 431.

swing may include analysis of movement and muscle activation patterns as well as internal and external forces."[21]

The Kinematic Chain

There are many different types of swings in golf, but they all have one thing in common: The golfer must employ a wide variety of muscles and body movements to perform them. Kinematics is the area of mechanics that focuses on the motion of an object. In golf biomechanics the kinematic chain refers to the different parts of the body and the muscles that are involved in producing a swing and to the transfer of muscular energy to the ball. Each movement in this chain adds to the overall energy of the swing to produce clubhead speed, which on contact with the ball produces the force that moves the ball. Each part of the swing must be done

The sequence of body movements that go into a golf swing, or the kinematic chain, determines the amount of force with which the club strikes the ball.

correctly in order to transfer maximum power to the ball so it goes where the golfer wants it to go.

There are four different parts in the swing: the address, also called the setup; the backswing, in which the golfer brings the club up and away from the ball; the downswing from the apex of the backswing until contact with the ball; and the follow-through as the club completes the swing after contact. The four parts of the swing use nearly every muscle and joint in the body, and they all require different movements. The task facing golfers is to combine them efficiently to produce the shots they desire.

In his book, *Golf RX*, Vijay Vad, a physician who specializes in sports medicine, explains the importance of a good golf swing:

> Proper sequencing [of the parts of the golf stroke] is the key to making a timely, powerful golf swing. [If] that sequence is broken [or] there's a glitch [error] in the kinematic chain, your ability to hit the ball solidly is greatly diminished. And there is very little room for error: Miss the center of the clubface by as little as a quarter of an inch, or even less, and you can find yourself in the trees with the chipmunks instead of in the fairway.[22]

The Address and the Backswing

The first part of any golf swing is the address, a static position at the start of the swing that golfers take over their ball, wherever the ball may be. In this prelude to the swing, golfers grip the club, bend their knees (usually 20 to 25 degrees), tilt their spinal angle to about 45 degrees vertically from the ground, place their feet apart (which for most shots is shoulder-width apart), and make other adjustments to their body, head, and hands. The head should be angled downward enough so the golfer can clearly see the ball but not so low as to nearly touch the chest, which can restrict the length of the backswing. At address, golfers place their clubhead directly behind the ball before beginning their swing. The many muscles and joints used in the address should be relaxed and free of tension.

A golfer rotates his body until he reaches the apex of his backswing in order to generate energy on the forward motion of his downswing.

Contributors to Swing Power

In his book, *The Science of Golf*, John Wesson calculates how much power various body parts and movements add to the power of a golf swing. To do this, Wesson had a golfer swing a driver several times using limited body movements. The player first used only wrists to hit the ball and then in succeeding swings added arms, the upper body, and then all body parts in a full swing. For each set of swings Wesson calculated clubhead speed, the best way to figure the energy the clubhead transmits to the ball on contact. His calculations show that wrists alone contribute 10 percent of the energy of the swing; wrists and arms 20 percent; wrists, arms, and upper body 40 percent; and the complete movement the full 100 percent. Wesson writes that his results "indicate that the wrists, arms, and upper body together provide less than half the energy transmitted to the clubhead, implying that the legs supply more than half the energy. This outcome might seem surprising because most players are more conscious of the arms than of the legs."

John Wesson. *The Science of Golf*. England: Oxford University Press, 2009, p. 148.

The whole of a golfer's body parts contribute to the power of his or her swing.

In the second part of the swing, the backswing, golfers swing the club up and away from the ball, twisting both sideways and back, so the club swings behind their body and above their head. The rotation of the hips, shoulders, and wrists and the muscles in the thighs, hips, shoulders, buttocks, and back are important contributors to the energy this part of the swing generates. An important key in the backswing is that the golfer's head should remain stationary over the ball. This forces the backswing to revolve directly around the spine, a motion that stretches the joints and muscles and better stores energy for the next part of the swing: the downswing.

The backswing lasts only about a second, but the average time for good players is 0.82 seconds. Despite its short duration, the backswing is vitally important to the overall swing, because the backswing correctly aligns the center of the golfer's body over the ball so that the golfer can generate power and hit the ball squarely.

The Downswing

The downswing, the third part of the golf swing, follows the backswing, and it allows golfers to create clubhead speed. The downswing is even shorter in duration than the backswing—only 0.23 seconds on average for top golfers driving the ball off a tee. The downswing has two parts. The first part is the movement at the top of the backswing to stop the club's upward momentum and begin the club's downward swing toward the ball. The second part is the continuous acceleration of the club along its intended path to the ball.

The moment in the swing in which golfers begin changing the direction of their club from up to down is an important point in the swing. Some golfers pause briefly at the top of their backswing before starting the downswing, while other golfers fluidly transition from the upward movement to the downward movement without stopping. Both ways can be successful. In their book, *Golf Anatomy*, Craig Davies and Vince DiSaia explain that this change in direction must be done carefully either way golfers choose to perform it. They write, "The transition from the upswing [the backswing] to the downswing requires great coordination by the athlete and an ability to separate the lower body and pelvis from the upper body."[23] According to Hume, Keogh, and Reid, the downward swing should begin by moving the lower body toward the ball, followed by the rest of the body, in order to ensure the most efficient transfer of power in the swing.

They write, "The kinetic chain action involves the initiation of the movement with the legs and hips followed by movement of the trunk and shoulders, and finally the hands and wrists. If [the downswing is] executed correctly, the amount of kinetic energy is greater than the sum of the parts."[24]

Using the legs and hips to initiate the downswing gets the weight of the entire body moving toward the ball, which allows golfers to generate maximum swing speed and produce a powerful force at the point when the clubhead contacts with the ball. The core muscles of the body in the chest, shoulders, hips, and abdomen along with muscles in the thighs and lower legs are important in the downswing to produce power.

The golfer uses this power to accelerate the club throughout the downswing to generate clubhead speed at impact. However, this acceleration should be gradual and should reach its peak at impact. Golfers who try to swing too fast early in the downswing often generate so much speed that they have trouble controlling the club and actually have to slow down to hit the ball, which is the opposite of what they should do. The momentum of the golfer and the clubhead should only be slowed during the final phase of the swing: the follow-through.

The Follow-Through

The fourth part of the golf swing is the follow-through. It begins after the ball has been struck and ends when the club finishes its trajectory through the swing path. Its purpose is to disperse all the power that the first three parts of the swing generated. Clubhead contact with the ball lasts only 0.0005 seconds. In that instant, the club immediately begins to lose speed as it delivers force to the ball. For example, a club swung at 100 miles per hour (161kmh) decreases to 90 miles per hour (145kmh) on contact. Despite this small loss of speed upon striking the ball, the clubhead and the body parts wielding it are still traveling at an extremely high rate of speed. In the follow-through the body's muscles work to decrease that speed and to bring the swing to a halt without injuring the golfer. Davies and DiSaia explain, "This phase of

Golf Horsepower

Horsepower is the name for several units of measurement of power from electrical to mechanical power. In his book, *The Physics of Golf*, physicist Theodore P. Jorgensen computes how much horsepower muscles supply to a golf swing. He writes,

> When the large muscles of the body are suitably loaded [stretched], they are capable of producing mechanical power through a single contraction of about one-eighth horsepower per pound. I have made a rough estimate of the power of a professional golfer during the standard swing and find that in part of the swing he delivers energy at about two horsepower. In the human body, for each muscle used to produce motion in one direction there is a muscle of about the same mass used to produce motion in the opposition direction. These considerations tell us that we should be looking for at least 32 pounds of muscle to supply the power for the golf swing.

Theodore P. Jorgensen. *The Physics of Golf,* 2nd ed. New York: Springer-Verlag, 1999, p. 4.

the golf swing is very taxing because the muscles must work predominantly through [opposing] contractions to slow down the body. The golfer's entire core [works] at maximum power to produce force and decelerate the body."[25]

The body's muscles work in pairs called extensors and flexors to move the body's joints and their attached parts. Extensors shorten muscles to increase the angle of body parts at the joint, while flexors lengthen to decrease the angle of body parts at the joint. This opposing muscle contraction occurs in muscle pairs when they perform any physical task. The flexors slow the swing by gradually lengthening hip, leg, body, and arm muscles to release the tension from the muscular contraction built up during the swing. The

The extension of Paula Creamer's body on her follow-through is indicative of the power generated by her swing.

follow-through arc of most elite golfers finishes so high that their hands may rotate around their neck. Follow-throughs of other golfers may be much shorter because they do not swing as hard and because of differences in body type and level of physical fitness that decrease the rotation of their swing. The follow-through is important in the golf swing, because if the golfer does not complete it properly, he or she could be injured.

A Two-Lever Action

Archimedes, a third-century Greek mathematician and inventor, once boasted, "Give me a place to stand and with a lever I will move the whole world."[26] A lever is a rigid bar that pivots on a fixed hinge. Levers increase a person's strength to allow them to move heavy objects they could not move otherwise. In analyzing the golf swing, scientists discovered that it contains two sets of levers that, when properly used, add power to the swing of any golfer. Levers can also act like pendulums, a term that refers to weights suspended from a pivot point that can swing freely. In his book, *Newton on the Tee*, John Zumerchik writes, "The golf swing is a double pendulum, or two-lever action. One lever formed by the shoulders, arms, and wrists, rotates around an axis in the upper chest; the second lever is the club rotating around an axis formed by the hands."[27]

In a two-lever, double-pendulum golf swing, a golfer begins with his arms straight down in front of him as he holds a golf club, forming a V shape. The player's arms form the first lever, and during the swing, they pivot around a point between the player's shoulders. The second lever is the club itself, which during the swing pivots about the player's wrists. The two levers can clearly be seen about halfway through the backswing. The arms are angled directly at the base of the club, as they are throughout the swing. At this point, the wrists are no longer straight but are angled with the club extending upward from them. This creates two lines of force for the two levers, one from the arms to the club and one from the club to the wrists. When the wrists are angled during the swing, they are considered cocked. The wrists straighten when the golfer hits the ball, which adds additional power to the swing from the energy created by uncocking the wrists. The two levers in the swing increase its speed, the truest indicator of swing power.

DOUBLE PENDULUM SWING

A golf swing is a two-lever, double pendulum swing. The golf club itself is a lever, and the shoulders, arms, and wrists act as another lever. Each lever pivots around its axis point like a pendulum, or in the case of two levers, a double pendulum. In the backswing, force, or energy, is generated by the two levers. In the downswing, the energy supplied by the two levers gives the power needed for an effective swing.

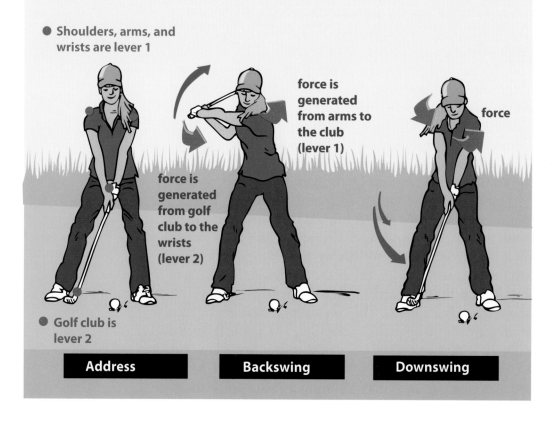

● Shoulders, arms, and wrists are lever 1

force is generated from arms to the club (lever 1)

force is generated from golf club to the wrists (lever 2)

force

● Golf club is lever 2

Address   **Backswing**   **Downswing**

A Pendulum-Like Swing

The effect of a two-lever, double-pendulum golf swing is also important in putting. During putting, however, a pendulum-like swing is key to accuracy and not power. One reason a pendulum-like swing is important to accurate putting is that

a pendulum swings back and forth in a straight line, which ensures that the head of the putter will squarely meet the ball at impact. As with full-swing shots, square contact in putting avoids sending the ball off in an unintended direction. In his book, *The Science of Golf*, John Wesson notes that proper contact is important to ensure that the correct amount of force the golfer wants to use is transferred to the ball. He writes, "[When] the ball is struck with a motion partly across the face of the putter, the sideways speed of the putter is only partially transmitted to the ball."[28] That happens because in mishits, the ball rolls up the clubface, reducing the power of the stroke.

Hitting a putt the same way every time is important. It allows a golfer to know how hard to hit putts of various lengths. A pendulum travels the same distance backward as it does forward, so having the putter mimic this motion helps golfers putt more accurately by helping them maintain

Golfers must practice to establish a consistency in the speed and tempo of their putting motion so that they can improve their accuracy.

HOLE IN ONE

Golfers have to know the physical strengths and weaknesses of their bodies so they can adapt their stroke to them.

a smooth, constant tempo in their putting motion. In an article on the website MeetingsNet, physicist and putting expert Dave Pelz explains,

Consider a pendulum: a mass suspended from a fixed point. If we start the pendulum swinging with a short arc, the mass will move slowly through its arc. The time it takes to travel through its arc is defined as its period. If we start the same pendulum with a longer arc, the mass will move more rapidly through its arc, but its period will be the same. It has the same time to travel a greater distance, so it moves faster."[29]

Challenges to a Proper Swing

As golfers perform a swing, their club travels in a wide arc around their body. The typical angle for the line of the swing is about 45 degrees from vertical and the average length the club travels both back and forward in a full swing is 28 feet (8.5m). Swinging a club correctly along a line that long to precisely hit a small object only 1.68 inches (4.27cm) in diameter is a daunting task. Wesson explains, "Amazingly, the clubhead [must] hit the ball within, say, half an inch of the center of the clubface. A required half-inch accuracy after a journey of 28 feet! It is probably best to dismiss such thoughts when you approach the swing."[30]

Another problem in learning to swing correctly is that most golf instruction adheres to basic swing elements, such as making a very full body turn, that not all golfers can perform the same way because everyone's body is different. Someone who is tall, for example, will not complete a swing the same way as someone who is short. In his book, *The Physics of Golf*, Theodore P. Jorgensen writes, "The limitations of the human body" must be considered a factor in the way people are able to swing a club. "Let us face the fact that our bodies are all different, and for this reason alone the style of the stroke that each of us may develop will be different from

the style of other golfers."[31] In other words, not everyone can execute a perfect swing. As a result, individual golfers have to figure out how to adapt the major principles of golf instruction to their abilities.

CHAPTER **4**

Training and Conditioning

American Tiger Woods, one of the greatest professional golfers, learned to play golf as a child. His father, Earl Woods, once boasted that Tiger knew how to swing a club before he could walk. When Tiger was only a few months old, Earl hit balls into a net in the family's garage, while Tiger watched from a high chair. Tiger's early introduction to golf continued when Earl took him to a driving range when he was eighteen months old and to a golf course before his third birthday.

While Tiger seemed to have a talent for playing golf, he still had to learn the intricacies of how to play the game. After his dad taught him the basics when he was a child, Tiger had a series of professional instructors who helped him refine his game. His search for the perfect swing led Tiger to totally revamp his swing several times during his professional career. In 2010, at age 34, Woods turned to golf instructor Sean Foley to help him improve his play, even though Woods had already won fourteen major tournaments, a feat that placed him second in golf history to legendary American golfer Jack Nicklaus, who won eighteen major titles before retiring in 2005.

Foley is a successful instructor because he understands that different people learn in different ways, so he uses a variety of instructional methods. He explains, "Teaching is really more a

Learning to Play Golf

The ease with which professionals smash long, straight drives or sink putts that curve wildly on their way to the hole, makes golf look simple. Golf, however, is hard to learn and to play, because the act of hitting a golf ball is extremely difficult, even though the ball is stationary, as opposed to a ball in baseball traveling at 90 miles per hour (145kmh) toward a batter. Luckily for would-be golfers, it is easy to find proper instruction on how to play golf. The best way is to take lessons from a professional teacher, but novice players can also read books, watch videos, and visit websites that offer valuable tips on the right way to swing and hit various shots. Because everyone learns in different ways, beginners have to decide the best way for them to learn to play. Good instruction from any source is

key to learning to play golf. However, people also need to practice and play a lot of golf once they learn the basics, so their body and brain can absorb their lessons. Even professional golfers must play regularly to maintain the quality of their game.

A young golfer gets putting advice from her instructor.

function of how people best learn things. If you have a player who has kind of an auditory sense to him, maybe you get him hitting balls wearing a blindfold and barefoot, listening to [classical music]. Whatever instills the lesson best."[32]

Although golfers learn to play by reading, watching videos, taking lessons, and practicing endlessly, everyone responds differently to various teaching methods and must choose the one that is right for him or her. When Greg Ditrinco, a snow skier who wanted to learn to play golf, started taking golf lessons, he had trouble understanding verbal instructions from the teacher. Fortunately for Ditrinco, his golf school filmed the students during their lessons and used the video as a teaching tool. Watching himself as he swung a golf club,

Ditrinco saw instantly what he was doing wrong. He says, "The video is where I begin to understand my 'set-up' problems. [Try] as I might to adjust . . . I'm struggling. But clear as day I see on the screen that my body is twisted like a pretzel, with the solution as obvious as tilting the other way."[33]

Training the Brain

Swinging a golf club is a physical act, but it is the brain that controls the physical movements that muscles make. Karl Morris, a psychologist who helps European professional golfers play better, says, "To actually change your swing you have to change your brain. You have to alter the neural pathways in your brain which send the commands to your muscles."[34] Brain plasticity is the quality the brain has to change, grow, alter its functions, and learn new things; even senior citizens can learn to play golf because the brain's ability to learn new things never ends.

The human brain can learn to perform physical actions in the same way time after time. Learning these types of skills is called motor learning. It allows people to perform

An instructor adjusts a student's body position and videotapes her practice for later viewing and analysis in order to help her refine the motor skills needed to improve her swing.

complicated physical activities, such as dancing, playing musical instruments, and playing golf. There are, however, many ways to learn motor skills. Lee McGinnis and Brian Glibkowski, professors at Stonehill College in Easton, Massachusetts, lead a team that studied the teaching methods of twenty-five of the finest golf instructors in the United States. The study, released in 2011, found there were three primary styles of learning: direct, relational, and analytical.

In direct learning students learn by following specific instructions, watching videos, or practicing an activity. In relational learning students learn from examples from other situations that are then applied to the subject they are learning, such as golf. In analytical learning students learn how and why they have to do something. As one golf instructor explains, "You have to help them [students] understand why the ball goes where it goes."[35] Since each person's brain processes information in different ways, some students may have more than one learning style and others may have just one. For this reason teachers use many different methods to teach.

Once students learn the basics of how to do something, they ingrain that knowledge on their brain through repetition by practicing and by playing. According to John J. Ratey in his book, *A User's Guide to the Brain*, when people learn new things, it actually changes their brain and how they command their body. He writes, "No one really understands how we learn to tie our shoes or play tennis. [Neuroscientists have] found that within the first 5 or 6 hours of practicing a new motor skill, the brain shifts the new instructions from short-term memory to the areas responsible for permanent motor skills. [And] the formula for the task was virtually hard-wired into the brain."[36]

As people learn new motor skills, the part of their brain known as the cerebellum absorbs the knowledge and controls the actions of the body. But not long after someone stops learning something new, this knowledge moves to the motor cortex, the part of the brain in the cerebral cortex that is key in planning, controlling, and executing voluntary movements. This new knowledge is stored there more or less permanently as muscle memory, a type of memory that helps people perform the same tasks again in the future.

Body Awareness

Even after people have learned new motor skills and the information is stored as muscle memory in the brain, they can continue to improve as they are exposed to new lessons on how to perform. This new knowledge enables their brains to refine the previously learned motor skills, such as driving or putting. Another way golfers improve is through the feedback their brains receive when they hit shots during practice or a game. During a golf stroke, whether a powerful drive or a feathery putt, muscles and body parts send signals to the brain about what is happening. The golfer's conscious mind can analyze this data and compare the current swing with past swings. This is especially true of very good and very bad shots. The sensory feedback golfers get from their muscles and body parts can help them correct

A golfer's awareness of the position and movement of body during his swing can help him better understand what changes he needs to make to generate power and improve accuracy.

mistakes. It can also confirm that they are swinging properly, which helps to ingrain the movement in their brain for future shots.

The brain function that allows people to feel how their body is functioning while hitting a golf ball is proprioception, which is more commonly called "body awareness." The word *proprioception* comes from two Latin words that mean "one's own" and "perception." It refers to the brain's ability to sense how well the body is performing a physical action. In their book, *Golf Anatomy*, Craig Davies and Vince DiSaia claim that golfers overlook the importance of proprioception in improving performance. They write, "[Proprioception is] the process by which the body can use muscles in immediate response to its surroundings. Your body must be able to respond rapidly to changing body positions and different forces throughout the swing. Imagine how many body parts are moving in different directions during the golf swing, all in less than [a few] seconds."[37]

Proprioception enables the brain to sense where the body's parts are at any given time during a swing. This allows a golfer to perform the movements that each shot requires. The brain does this through receptors in the muscles and joints that track every movement they are making. The information is then relayed to the brain. The brain combines the data so a player knows what is happening and can control his or her swing.

The ability golfers have to do this is often referred to as being able to "feel the swing." Although everyone has this ability, some golfers are able to sense and understand this feedback more precisely than other golfers. This heightened body awareness enables them to more easily understand what they are doing, so they can more easily correct their swing when necessary. Golfers who can easily use body awareness to correct the way they play are called "feel players." Golfers who have more trouble sensing what is wrong with their swings must depend more heavily on instructional tips to correct swing flaws and are called "mechanical players." Either way of learning golf is fine and can produce excellent players.

Golf Fitness

When Woods became a professional golfer in 1996, after winning his third straight U.S. Amateur Championship, most of the world's best golfers were not overly concerned about physical fitness. Even though the professional tour provided a portable training facility that traveled from tournament to tournament, not many players used it. "There was no one in the gym. There was just me,"[38] says Woods. But after Woods rapidly ascended to number one in the ranking of the world's best golfers, other players noticed his devotion to fitness and realized they needed to get in better physical shape to compete

Tiger Woods includes running as part of his fitness regimen in order to improve his aerobic endurance.

Tiger Woods on Fitness

Superb physical fitness is one reason American professional golfer Tiger Woods has become, in the eyes of many, the greatest golfer ever. Woods has remained muscular and athletic as he has aged because he works out so hard. According to TigerWoods.com, this is Woods's daily physical fitness routine:

6:30 a.m.: One hour of cardio. Choice between endurance runs, sprints, or biking.

7:30 a.m.: One hour of lower weight training. 60–70 percent of normal lifting weight, high reps and multiple sets.

8:30 a.m.: High protein/low-fat breakfast. Typically includes egg-white omelet with vegetables.

9:00 a.m.: Two hours on the golf course. Hit on the range and work on swing.

11:00 a.m.: Practice putting for 30 minutes to an hour.

Noon: Play nine holes.

1:30 p.m.: High protein/low-fat lunch. Typically includes grilled chicken or fish, salad and vegetables.

2:00 p.m.: Three-to-four hours on the golf course. Work on swing, short game and occasionally play another nine holes.

6:30 p.m.: 30 minutes of upper weight training. High reps.

7:00 p.m.: Dinner and rest.

TigerWoods.com. "Health & Fitness: Tiger's Daily Routine." TigerWoods.com. http://web.tigerwoods.com/fitness/tigerDailyRoutine.

against him. Today most golfers, professional or amateur, work out regularly; some professionals even travel with their own personal trainers.

When Woods began his professional career at the age of twenty, he carried only 158 pounds (72kg) on his skinny 6-foot, 1-inch frame. But through workouts and the natural maturation of his body over the next few years,

Woods gained almost 30 pounds (14kg), almost all of it muscle. Weight lifting helped Woods become more powerful, and many other golfers also lift weights so they can build muscle to increase their swing speed and hit the ball farther. Every increase in speed of 1 mile per hour (1.6 kmh) sends a golf ball an additional 3 yards (2.7m) farther.

Weight lifting, however, is not as important in golf as it is in sports such as football, where athletes need brute power to be successful. In golf it is more important for golfers to condition their bodies to be flexible and balanced, because one of the key elements in golf fitness is the range of motion of the joints in the body, such as those in the shoulders and knees. A lack of flexibility will limit the range of movement of muscles and body parts when golfers swing. According to Davies and DiSaia, limited flexibility makes it hard for people to play and even to learn how to hit the ball properly. They write, "Each joint in your body has a range of motion that is specific to you. [Some] people have greater mobility, and some are limited in their range of movement. The problem is, when learning to hit the ball better, many people try to move into positions [in the swing] that aren't physically possible [for them] because of limitations in range of motion."[39]

Because flexibility is important in golf, most golfers incorporate stretching into their exercise routines. They also do a lot of stretching before they play or practice to loosen their muscles. This preplay stretching is not for just a few seconds, either. Before Woods practices or plays, he stretches for up to forty minutes in a routine that includes working his spine and all of his joints, including his toes. This stretching allows Woods to completely unleash his power in each swing. When Woods lifts weights, he does not lift to build strength as athletes do in many other sports. Instead, he lifts to build muscular endurance. Woods says, "My weight-training program is designed for balance, control and endurance. I lift to enhance my entire body because golf requires upper and lower symmetry. I also develop my right and left sides equally because it improves how I strike the ball."[40]

To increase his aerobic endurance, Woods likes to run or ride a bike. And like most golfers, he does a lot of work to strengthen his core—his abdominal, hip, and back muscles—because they are vital in executing swings. Woods also plays golf almost daily, not just to practice hitting shots, but also to strengthen all of the muscles involved in golf so they will not tire during a tournament.

Injuries

In June 2008 Woods won the U.S. Open, and he did it on a broken leg and an injured knee. It was only after his victory—one of the grittiest and most spectacular in golf history—that the public found out about his injuries. Woods admitted he had two stress fractures to the tibia of his left leg and a torn

A golf swing extends and rotates the spine, a motion that can cause injury to the vertebra with repetition over time.

Golf Injuries

In his book, *Golf RX: A 15-Minute-a-Day Core Program for More Yards and Less Pain*, Vijay Vad, a physician who specializes in sports medicine, explains that most golf injuries occur from playing a lot, which he defines as more than fifty rounds a year, and from being in poor physical condition. He writes,

> The addiction to the game can be dangerous if your body is not conditioned to play so much golf. The majority of golf injuries—approximately 80 percent—are overuse injuries. These injuries are mostly seen in the back, but they can also occur in the shoulder, elbow, hip, and knee. The underlying cause of these injuries is a loss of flexibility, strength, and endurance in your core muscle group. [Improper] swing technique is the second biggest cause of golf injuries. An abbreviated finish or sudden stop (rapid deceleration) of the club can cause harm to the wrists, elbows, shoulders hips, and back.

Vijay Vad with Dave Allen. *Golf RX: A 15-Minute-a-Day Core Program for More Yards and Less Pain*. New York: Gotham, 2007, pp. 167–168.

anterior cruciate ligament (ACL) that required reconstructive surgery. He was in pain during the tournament, but he was determined to continue. After he won, Woods declared the tournament, "My greatest ever championship."[41]

Even though golf is a low-impact sport compared to football, hockey, and soccer, which involve high-speed collisions between players, golfers can still suffer a variety of injuries. Most golf injuries affect the back and joints in the shoulders, elbows, wrists, hips, knees, and ankles. One cause of injury is the force that golfers generate when they swing hard, which is sometimes as much as eight times their body weight; for someone weighing 200 pounds (91kg), that force equals 1,600 pounds (726kg). That tremendous force is hardest on a golfer's back and knees. Woods, for instance, has an extremely powerful swing, and his 2008 knee surgery was not the first or last time he required surgery for his left knee. In a right-handed golfer, such as Woods, the left knee bears the weight of the swing on impact; for a left-hander, the right knee is the one most affected. Swings can also injure golfers by forcing the trunk of the body to rotate too severely and both shoulders to execute a wide range of motions. The risk of injury is increased because this twisting and turning occur at high speeds.

The effect of one swing will not usually cause an injury. But over time thousands of swings can weaken and damage joints, muscles, and ligaments. The hips are also vulnerable. Because they play so much, many professional golfers have had hip replacement surgery, including Jack Nicklaus. Golfers also suffer a variety of back injuries, some of them from the follow-through part of the swing. The most common injuries are to muscles in the back and side of the body. People who play a lot of golf can also suffer damage to the vertebra in their spinal cord from the cumulative effect of swinging a club thousands of times. Injuries to the wrist, knee, and shoulder are also common.

The best way to prevent golf injuries is to be in good physical shape and to swing correctly. However, even physically fit professional golfers can be injured from swinging a club over and over again. Many amateur golfers injure themselves because their swings are faulty. In his book, *Newton on the Tee*, John Zumerchik explains why bad swings can injure golfers: "An unbalanced or nonfluid swing creates uneven stresses that aren't well distributed throughout the body, which can lead to an injury. If you don't have a smooth swing [there is] too much pushing or pulling going on somewhere, too many of your muscles are fighting each other."[42]

In addition to being in shape and swinging the right way, stretching before playing or practicing greatly decreases the chance of injury. Stretching increases the blood flow

HOLE IN ONE

The oldest golfer to win a men's major championship is Julius Boros who, at age 48, won the 1968 PGA Championship. The next oldest is Jack Nicklaus who won the 1986 Masters at age 46.

to muscles which makes them more pliable and thus less susceptible to injury.

A Game for Life

In most sports athletes are unable to perform at a high level past the age of forty. Golf, however, is an exception. In his book, *Golf RX*, Vijay Vad, a physician who specializes in sports medicine, writes, "The thing I most admire about golf is that it's a lifetime recreational activity, one you can enjoy well into your later years if you stay healthy. In that sense, there's no other sport like it."[43]

The fact that older people can still play golf at a high level is evident in the Champions Tour, a series of tournaments every year for male players over the age of fifty, and the Legends Tour for women over forty-five. Some golfers on that senior tour remain competitive for years, even winning tournaments in their sixties when they are more than a decade older than their competitors.

CHAPTER 5

Golf Psychology

P eople have been battling each other in athletic contests for thousands of years. Chuang-tzu, a Chinese philosopher who lived in the fourth century B.C., observed how the pressure of competition can affect athletes. He writes, "When an archer is shooting for nothing, he has all his skill. If he shoots for a brass buckle, he is already nervous. If he shoots for a prize of gold, he goes blind or sees two targets—He is out of his mind! His skill has not changed. But the prize divides him. He cares. He thinks more of winning than of shooting—And the need to win drains him of power."[44] Chuang-tzu focuses on a key challenge in sports: controlling emotion. Since athletes have a fierce desire to perform well and to win, they can experience powerful feelings that can make it hard for them to do their best.

Emotions in Golf

Psychology is the scientific study of how the human mind controls behavior. Sports psychology is the branch of psychology that focuses on how the mind functions during athletic performance. Jim Taylor is a psychologist who believes that to win, athletes must control their thoughts and feelings during competition. In an article for *Psychology Today* magazine he writes, "Emotions will ultimately dictate how you perform throughout a competition. Emotions during a competition can cover the spectrum from excitement and elation

A Lonely Sport

Unlike team sports, such as baseball and football, golf is an individual sport. Although professional golfers have a caddy (a person who carries the golfer's clubs) who gives them advice, most pros rely entirely on themselves to win a match or tournament or to just play as well as they can. When players in team sports make mistakes, teammates can boost their spirits by telling them they will do better next time. But when professional golfers hit bad shots, there is no one to console them or cheer them up. Unless golfers do something to alleviate their anger or despair about the shot, they can carry those negative emotions with them as they walk or ride to their ball to hit their next shot. An eighteen-hole round of golf can take five hours. For much of that time a golfer is alone; his or her only companions are the thoughts

and emotions swirling around in their head. If golfers cannot control their minds, negative thoughts and feelings about how they are playing can erode their confidence and lead to more poor play. Outside of professional golf tournaments, golf is typically played with two to four players per hole who stay together for the entire round of golf (either nine or eighteen holes). However, even when playing with friends, golfers can be hundreds of yards away from them, and the lonely nature of golf makes it even more difficult mentally and psychologically than many other sports.

The isolation a golfer experiences on the course can affect the mental aspect of her game.

to frustration, anger, and disappointment. Emotions are often strong and, most troublesome, they can linger and hurt your performances long after you first experience them."[45]

Golfers, even poor golfers, often hit the ball confidently on the practice range, because they are mentally and physically relaxed. However, the pleasurable anticipation of playing a game they love often evaporates when golfers tee up their ball on the first hole. In what is known as "first-tee jitters," many golfers become nervous because they know that every stroke they make will now be added to their score. So golfers who swing easily and hit good shots while warming up may suffer weak opening drives or hit balls that sail right or left into water or sand traps once the game begins. Even American professional golfer Tiger Woods is not immune to first-tee trouble. On August 28, 2010, he had a triple bogey (3 over par) 7 on his first hole in the third round of the Barclays tournament.

First-tee nerves often disappear after the first stroke, whether good or bad, but the rest of the round can still be an emotional roller coaster. Each and every time a golfer hits a ball, he or she will experience joy, despair, anger, and other powerful emotions, depending on how well, or how badly, the shots turn out.

The Stress of Golf

More bad things than good things can happen when a golfer strikes a ball. Even the world's best golfers hit poor shots that land in trouble spots that make their next shot more difficult. Sometimes their next shot is so difficult that golfers may need an extra stroke or even multiple strokes to finish the hole. Such terrible shots can make golfers feel angry about the costly mistake and fearful that the mishit will hurt their chance of winning. Those errors can also make golfers lose confidence in their ability, which makes it more difficult for them to hit succeeding shots.

Although most golfers have enough faith in their skill to ignore negative emotions after hitting one bad shot, some players have trouble controlling their anger, disappointment, or lack of confidence. American professional golfer Jack Nicklaus says, "It takes hundreds of good golf shots to gain confidence but only one bad shot to lose it."[46] Some golfers remain focused on their mistake and are unable to concentrate on their next shot. They begin to fear they will hit another bad one, and many do, which fills their mind with more negative thoughts and makes hitting the next shot even harder.

Negative thoughts and emotions create stress, which in turn can induce a physiological reaction known as "fight or

When the brain perceives stress, it activates body systems that produce hormones (blue and yellow arrows) that increase heart rate and muscle tension and sap the body's energy.

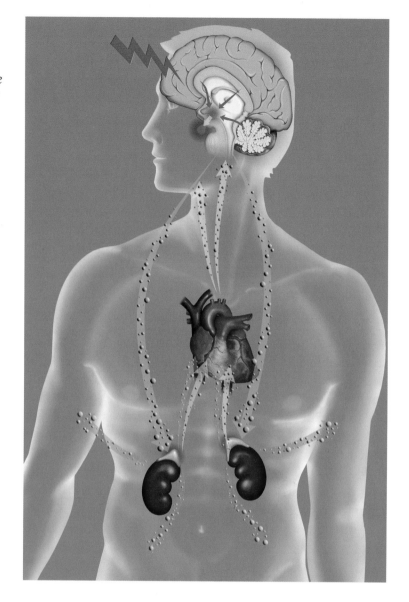

flight." Physician Neil F. Neimark studied the connections between the mind and body to help his patients become healthier. He writes, "[The flight-or-fight] response is hardwired into our brains and represents a genetic wisdom designed to protect us from bodily harm."[47] This instinctive physical response to stressful situations originally helped primitive people prepare to either flee from danger or to stand their ground and fight. However, strong emotions that

The Power of Negative Emotions

Jim Taylor, a psychologist who helps golfers deal with their emotions, says that athletes must learn to control their emotions in order to perform to the best of their ability in golf and other sports because negative emotions affect people both physically and mentally. In an article for *Psychology Today* magazine, Taylor writes,

> With frustration and anger, your intensity goes up and leads to muscle tension, breathing difficulties, and a loss of coordination. It also saps your energy and causes you to tire quickly. . . . Negative emotions can also hurt you mentally. Your emotions are telling you that, deep down, you're not confident in your ability to perform well and achieve your competitive goals. Your confidence will decline and you will have negative thoughts to go along with your negative emotions. Also, since your negative emotions are so strong, you will likely have difficulty focusing on what will help you to perform well; the negative emotions draw your attention onto all of the negative aspects of your performance. Finally, negative emotions can hurt your motivation to perform because you just don't feel good and it's no longer fun.

Jim Taylor. "Sports: The Power of Emotions." *Psychology Today*, December 1, 2010. www.psychologytoday.com/blog/the-power-prime/201012/sports-the-power-emotions.

produce mental stress, such as anger, fear, and anxiety, can also ignite a fight-or-flight response, even when people are not in any physical danger.

The fight-or-flight response releases adrenaline, noradrenaline, cortisol, and other chemicals into the bloodstream, increasing the respiratory rate and sharpening eyesight. They also increase blood flow to muscles and limbs, tightening them in preparation for action and quickening the brain's impulses to a person's muscles. These physical changes weaken golfers by using energy they need to continue playing. Psychologically, the response exaggerates fear in the mind and makes a person hunt for possible dangers. This focus on fear and danger makes it hard for people to think positively and make good decisions. These fight-or-flight changes negatively affect golfers, because they need to be relaxed mentally and physically to play well.

Stress during key moments in a round of golf can also trigger a fight-or-flight response in golfers; their muscles become tense, they start to sweat, and they may have trouble focusing on hitting their shot. An example is a golfer who is about to putt on the final hole during a tournament; if he is successful, he will win. Under other circumstances, the golfer would take one look at the hole and then quickly putt. Under the stress of competition, however, the golfer may spend several minutes agonizing over how to hit the putt, because a mix of emotions is confusing him. When the golfer finally putts, his stroke may be quicker, slower, or longer than usual, a physical sign that his body and mind are stressed. As a result, many golfers often miss those important putts.

Coping with emotions and stress is one of the most important things golfers need to learn to be successful. Golfers and sports psychologists have created many ways to help golfers deal with these challenges.

Dealing with Stress

Bob Rotella, one of the world's top sports psychologists, has helped many golfers learn to deal with stress to improve their play. One is American professional golfer Tom Kite, who won nineteen Professional Golf Association (PGA) Tour events, including the 1993 U.S. Open. Kite credits Rotella with helping him learn to ignore negative thoughts and think more positively. One way Rotella did that was to teach Kite not to obsess about a bad shot, because even the world's best players will occasionally make one. In his book, *Golf Is Not a Game of Perfect*, Rotella writes, "One of the things Tom, or

any successful pro, does best is to accept his bad shots, shrug them off, and concentrate completely on the next one. He has accepted the fact that, as he puts it, 'Golf is not a game of perfect.'"[48]

To eliminate any mental damage from their bad shots, golfers have to learn to put them out of their mind. Players refer to this tactic as "selective amnesia." American professional golfer Steve Stricker has won twenty professional tournaments and has consistently been ranked among the world's top ten players. Stricker believes his ability to forget errant shots and missed putts has been key to his success. He says, "[Golf is] a game of mistakes. It's a game of misses. And if you dwell on those misses and mistakes, you're not going anywhere. I've been able to do that over my career, to get that stuff out of my mind and move forward."[49]

Sports psychologist Bob Rotella, right, advises Henrik Stenson during a U.S. Open practice round in 2009. Many golfers consult sports psychologists in order to improve the mental part of their game.

Focusing on Each Shot

After American Bubba Watson won the 2012 Masters Tournament, a reporter asked, "What did you most overcome today?" Watson replied, "Thoughts that weren't on the golf course; thoughts that were about other things."[50] In other words, Watson won because he focused on hitting the best shot he could every time he struck his ball.

One way golfers focus their mind solely on playing is to develop a preshot routine, a series of steps that they complete before every shot. Performing a routine helps golfers eliminate unwanted thoughts and focus on the shot. The familiar actions can also help calm them in stressful situations. Woods has a preshot routine that he performs before every shot. He claims it is a big reason why he won so many tournaments. He says, "Great players operate 'in the moment.'

Jack Nicklaus credits his ability to visualize the details of his game as he prepares to make a shot as a key to his success on the course.

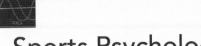

Sports Psychology

Sports psychologists help people perform better in athletic competition. Sports psychology is a relatively new career field, but it is growing as more athletes, both professional and amateur, realize that controlling their mind is key to performing well. Today at least twenty major U.S. colleges have a sports psychologist as a member of the staff and another seventy hire them as consultants. Many professional teams and individual athletes also work with psychologists to improve performance. Salaries for sports psychologists can top one hundred thousand dollars annually, depending on their clients. They can also earn money by writing books, giving speeches, or operating websites. In addition to having a degree in psychology, most sports psychologists are also current or former athletes themselves. Working with athletes can be exciting, but Scott Goldman, director of clinical and sport psychology at the University of Arizona, says the biggest reward is seeing how his athletes improve: "It's really rewarding to be part of this and watch the athletes shine after all the hard work they've done."

Quoted in Rebecca Voelker. "Hot Careers: Sport Psychology." American Psychological Association, November 2012. www.apa.org/gradpsych/2012/11/sport-psychology.aspx.

[My routine] helps me remain calm and in the present, prepared to execute a shot to the best of my ability."[51] Woods begins by standing behind his ball to look at his target, the area where he wants his ball to land. He then positions himself over his ball and waggles the club a few times to take tension out of his muscles. After looking at the target one last time, Woods strikes the ball.

Woods's preshot routine also includes visualization, a psychological technique, also known as mental imaging or mental rehearsal. In visualization a person mentally pictures, or rehearses, the action he or she is about to perform, including the desired outcome. Athletes in all sports use this method to enhance their performance. Golfers typically picture in their mind how they will strike their ball and how the ball will react. Nicklaus believes in visualization so much that he even does it while practicing. He says, "First I 'see' the ball where I want it to finish, nice and white and sitting up high on bright green grass. Then the scene quickly changes and I 'see' the ball going there: its path, trajectory and shape, even its behavior on landing."[52]

According to science writer John Zumerchik, visualization actually changes the brain and makes it easier for the brain and muscles to work together. In his book, *Newton on the Tee*, he writes, "Visualization makes the connection between nerves and the muscles they control grow stronger, from the motor cortex of the brain [which controls physical action] outward to the peripheral nervous system."[53] This increased connection also helps golfers swing faster and with more power.

Blocking Distractions

Even when golfers are able to control their own thoughts and emotions, other distractions on the golf course can disrupt their concentration. For example, planes flying overhead, traffic on nearby streets, and other people on the course can break the focus of even the best golfers. Woods is famous for stopping in midswing during tournaments, because he is distracted by the clicking sounds coming from the cameras of the spectators. Losing focus during a game is hard physically and mentally, and many golfers unnerved by a distracting noise often hit poor shots.

Since golfers usually play golf with other people and some use a caddy, golfers have to learn to block out anything other people say or do while they are playing. This is especially true in competition when some golfers intentionally try to distract their opponents so they will mishit the

ball. In trying to make his son mentally tougher than any other golfer, Earl Woods did a variety of things to try and distract Tiger when he was practicing. Earl says, "I dropped a bag of clubs at the impact of his swing. I imitated a crow's voice while he was stroking a putt. I would cough as he was taking the club back. I would say, 'Don't hit it in the water.' Those were the *nice* things I did. In other words I played with his mind."[54]

Tiger Woods approaches the tee surrounded by hundreds of fans during a Masters practice round in 2010. Golfers must learn to block noise, movement, and other distractions in order to be successful on the course.

The Zone

In January 2007 when Woods won the Buick Invitational in San Diego, California, it was his seventh straight victory. Winning that many tournaments in a row is an amazing feat. Only one person in the history of golf has more wins in a row than Woods: American golf legend Byron Nelson, who won eleven tournaments in a row in 1945. American professional golfer Bart Bryant marvels that Woods is able to play so well. He

HOLE IN ONE

Two tips from a sports pschologist to keep nerves from interfering with your golf game: 1. Take long, deep, slow breaths before making your shot. This will calm the brain and slow down racing thoughts. 2. Gently squeeze a golf ball in your hand for a few seconds then release. Squeeze the ball once again only more firmly, then release. This brings blood flow to the hands thus improving the feel of the club in your hands.

says, "You can't even hardly fathom it. It's just incredible. What he did is another evidence of the weird zone he's in. And he's been in it his whole life."[55] The zone that Bryant refers to is the almost mystical state of excellence athletes sometimes enter that helps them perform at optimum levels for extended periods. Golfers in the zone can perform seemingly impossible feats, such as having a one-under par birdie on nine straight holes, which is what American professional golfer Mark Calcavecchia did in 2009 at the Canadian Open, setting a PGA Tour record. Another example is shooting a score of 59 for eighteen holes (with the typical championship golf course being a par 72), a feat only five professional players have ever recorded.

In 1999 Janet A. Young and Michelle D. Pain, researchers at Monash University in Melbourne, Australia, asked athletes what it felt like to be in the zone. They discovered that athletes from different sports used similar terms to explain the experience. In their report they write, "Athletes describe salient features of the experience—total concentration and involvement, control, a unity of mind and body and a sense of personal fulfillment at an optimal level of performance—with remarkable similarity when asked to reflect on how it feels when their experiences are most positive."[56]

American professional golfer Sam Snead's experience of being in the zone conforms to data from Young and Pain's research. He explains, "When you're in the zone you feel more relaxed. Everything feels smooth. Your senses become sharper. You see all things more clearly. [You're] not trying to hit the shot, you just do it. [You] never feel as if you can't do what your mind is telling you to do."[57]

According to sports psychologist Jim Fannin, athletes enter the zone due to a heightened sense of mental and physical awareness and that feeling arises from players being unnaturally focused on their play, coupled with a sense of relaxation that takes away any fears about performing poorly. When he speaks to golfers, he says, "Your minds are in chaos, which means your golf games are, too. . . . [Champions] focus on what they want, not their fears. . . . Champions clear their minds and focus on the present. That's how you get in the zone, where you hit great shots without thinking."[58]

Choking

The opposite of being in the zone for golfers is to be in a mental state known as "choking." University of Chicago psychology professor Sian Beilock defines choking as "poor performance that occurs in response to the perceived stress of a situation."[59] Every golfer sometimes hits a bad shot at a key time, but players who repeatedly struggle to perform well in key moments are labeled "chokers," because their mistakes seem linked to their inability to control their emotions during competition. There are several reasons why stress causes people to choke. In addition to making it hard to focus, competitive stress can make athletes think too much about physical actions they usually perform automatically. This mental state is known as "paralysis by analysis." It disrupts players' ability to relax and allow their ingrained motor memories of how they performed in the past to guide their muscles. In their book, *Choke*, Beilock and Tiffany O'Callaghan write,

> Working memory is our mental scratch pad, the cognitive horsepower that allows us to focus on things that are relevant to solving a problem or task, and to ignore less relevant things. In stressful situations, the ability of working memory to direct attention to what's relevant is compromised. A computer is a good analogy. If you're running lots of programs at once, everything slows down. If you add worry to the mix, the attention needed to focus on the task can go awry.[60]

Once golfers begin choking, it can be hard for them to stop. In 1996 Australian professional golfer Greg Norman

Greg Norman reacts to a missed shot during the 1996 Masters, at which he blew a six-stroke lead going into the final round.

had a six-stroke lead going into the final round of the Masters Tournament, but he played horribly in the opening holes and failed to stop hitting bad shots the rest of the round. When Norman lost to Briton Nick Faldo, he was called a choker.

Golfers choke because they are not mentally strong enough to eliminate negative thoughts and to focus on hitting good shots. One reason Woods has won so many tournaments—seventy-nine PGA events through 2013—is that he is able to banish his negative thoughts. Sometimes he concentrates so hard on hitting a shot that he does not even remember striking the ball. He explains, "I tend to have these blackout moments where [I] know I was there but I don't remember performing the golf shot. I get so entrenched in the moment I guess my subconscious takes over. It's a weird thing."[61]

CHAPTER 6

Golf Technology

A merican Bobby Jones was one of the greatest amateur players in the history of golf. Even though he was an amateur, Jones regularly defeated professional golfers from 1923 to 1930, and in 1930 he won the professional U.S. Open and British Open championships and the U.S. Amateur and British Amateur tournaments, a historic feat nicknamed the Grand Slam. Jones retired from competitive golf in 1930 at the age of twenty-eight and cofounded Augusta National Golf Club in Augusta, Georgia, and helped to design its golf course. Three years later Jones started the Augusta National Invitation Tournament, which was later renamed the Masters Tournament. It became one of golf's four major tournaments. In 1965 American Jack Nicklaus won the Masters with a record score of 17 under par 271. Jones was so awed by how far Nicklaus hit the ball that he famously said, "Jack is playing a different game, a game with which I'm not familiar."[62] During his career, Jones had played with clubs fitted with hickory shafts, while Nicklaus used steel shafts, new technology that helped him hit the ball farther.

In 1997 Tiger Woods broke Nicklaus's record of 17 under par 271 by a stroke to become the first African American and the youngest player to ever win the Masters. Woods hit the ball so far and so straight that Sweden's Jesper Parnevik, who finished 19 strokes behind Woods, said, "Unless they build Tiger tees about 50 yards back, he's going to

The Moon Club

On February 6, 1971, American astronaut Alan Shepard (1923–1998) made the most famous golf swing in history: He was on the moon at the time. An avid golfer, Shepard hit a ball on the moon to demonstrate how low gravity affects a familiar physical act. In a scene televised back to Earth, Shepard hit two balls with a six-iron head attached to a metal instrument designed to collect moon rock and soil samples. Shepard said his space suit and thick gloves made it difficult to hit the balls: "It was impossible to get two hands on the handle [he used just one hand]. And it's impossible to make any kind of a turn. I shanked [badly mis-hit] the first one; it rolled into a crater about 40 yards away. The second one, I kept my head down." That second shot flew about 200 yards (183m), farther than a golfer could hit such a shot on Earth.

Quoted in Rod Driscoll. "Museum Moment: Mission Accomplished: Shepard's 'Moon Club' Brought Golf to Lofty Heights." USGA Museum, February 3, 2011. www.usgamuseum.com/about_museum/news_events/news_article.aspx?newsid=177.

Alan Shepard holds a makeshift club in order to play golf on the moon during the Apollo 14 mission in 1971.

win the next 20 of these."[63] Technological advancements helped Woods break Nicklaus's record: His driver had a larger head and was made of graphite compared to the steel one Nicklaus used.

The record-setting performances by Nicklaus in 1965 and by Woods in 1997 are dramatic historical evidence of how technology has affected the game of golf. In the six centuries since people began playing golf in Scotland, technological advances have created improvements in clubs that have made it easier for golfers, even bad golfers, to hit better and longer shots. Nothing, however, has changed the game more than technological advancements to golf's most basic piece of equipment—the ball.

Wood, Feathers, and Tree Sap

The first golf balls were carved out of wood, and players could not hit them more than 100 yards (91m). In the seventeenth century golfers began playing with featheries, leather pouches stuffed tight with bird feathers. They were superior in flight to wood balls, and most golfers could hit a feathery about 150 yards (137m). In the nineteenth century gutta–percha, a tough substance similar to rubber, revolutionized golf. Gutta-percha is sap from several types of Malaysian

WHY ARE GOLF BALLS DIMPLED?

In physics, the way dimples affect ball flight is called the "Magnus effect." Dimpled golf balls allow the ball to travel farther and straighter in the air than if the balls were smooth. Here's why: The dimples trap air, which increases spin. That increased spin also provides greater speed, which helps the ball stay in the air longer, and reduces drag, which is the force that slows balls down and shortens their flight.

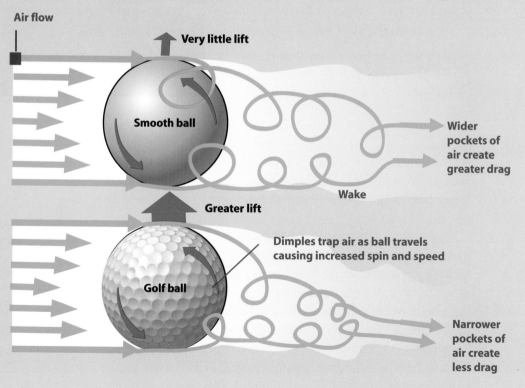

trees. The sap hardens when exposed to air, so people originally wrapped it around fragile items to protect them during shipping. In 1848 when St. Andrews University professor Robert Adams Preston received a marble statue wrapped in the hardened sap, he used the sap to make golf balls. Even though the sap balls did not travel as far as featheries, they soon became popular because they were cheaper to make and more durable; featheries could burst open when powerfully struck.

As more golfers began using the new balls, they discovered something strange. As the balls became worn and lost their smooth exterior, they flew straighter and farther than ever. Golfers began roughing up their balls before they used them and making new ones covered with tiny raised bumps called brambles. In 1905 English inventor William Taylor patented a golf ball that featured concave dimples, a design element that revolutionized the ball and is still used today.

Golf balls with concave dimples fly farther and straighter, because the dimples increase spin by trapping air that rolls over them as the balls travel through the air. In his book, *Newton on the Tee*, John Zumerchik writes, "According to [Sir Isaac] Newton's Third Law [of motion], the air must, in turn, create an upward lifting force on the ball."[64] The increased spin also provides greater speed, which helps the ball stay in the air longer and reduces drag, the force that slows the ball down and shortens its flight. In physics the way dimples affect ball flight is called the Magnus effect, named for German chemist and physicist Heinrich Gustav Magnus, who discovered it in 1853. The dimples trap air, thus causing the ball to spin more and move through the air more easily. Most modern golf balls made in the United States have 336 dimples, while those made in Great Britain have 330, and some can have as many as 500. Dimple patterns vary according to the manufacturer.

The United States Golf Association (USGA) once performed a test to see how much dimples affected distance when struck at 110 miles per hour (177kmh) by a club powered by

HOLE IN ONE

366 yards
The longest golf drive ever recorded with a feathery.

a machine. A perfectly smooth ball traveled about 130 yards (119m), far less than the 285 yards (261m) a golfer swinging that fast could propel a dimpled ball. In a game where ball flight and distance are important (except for the putting phase), a dimpled ball has the clear advantage.

Modern Golf Balls

In 1898 Coburn Haskell of Cleveland, Ohio, went to Akron, Ohio, to play golf with Bertram Work, superintendent of the B.F. Goodrich tire plant. While waiting for Work at the tire plant, Haskell wound rubber thread into a ball. Haskell was amazed when he bounced the ball, and it flew nearly to the ceiling. When Haskell told Work about his experience, Work suggested they make a ball with a rubber core covered with a thin layer of gutta-percha. Thus, the Haskell, the first modern golf ball, was born. Golf had only recently been introduced to the United States, and Haskell helped popularize it by making

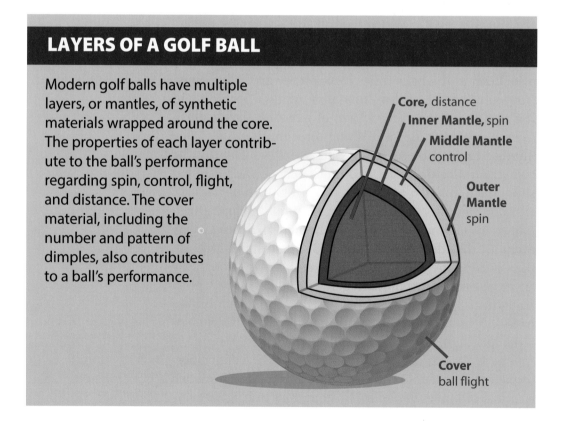

LAYERS OF A GOLF BALL

Modern golf balls have multiple layers, or mantles, of synthetic materials wrapped around the core. The properties of each layer contribute to the ball's performance regarding spin, control, flight, and distance. The cover material, including the number and pattern of dimples, also contributes to a ball's performance.

Core, distance
Inner Mantle, spin
Middle Mantle control
Outer Mantle spin
Cover ball flight

Launch Monitors

The many technological innovations in golf clubs have made playing golf easier. However, it has become much harder for golfers to choose clubs that will help them play their best, because clubs today are built from a variety of different materials and have so many different design features. Launch monitors, however, can make it easier for golfers to select the clubs that are right for them. When someone hits a ball, a launch monitor can measure vital factors, such as ball speed, launch angle (the initial angle of the ball's flight when it is struck), and backspin. Although golfers can buy a launch monitor of their own, most people use those provided for use in sporting goods stores so they can test a variety of clubs to see which ones are the best for them. Golfers hit balls into a screen which, when struck by the ball, shows data on the shot they hit, including how far it went and whether it flew straight or wandered left or right. The data helps golfers choose details in the club that will be best for them, such as the degree of its loft, which refers to the angle of the club's face.

it easier to play. In his book, *The Story of American Golf*, golf historian Herbert Warren Wind writes, "Now the game was really enjoyable for the weekend player. Now it only took one whistling drive with the rubber-cored ball to convert [someone to golf]."[65]

Today there is a great variation in golf balls, although all balls have to conform to the size mandated by the United States Golf Association (USGA): a diameter of 1.7 inches (4.3cm) and a weight of no more than 1.6 ounces (45.4gm). Although most modern balls still have a rubber core like the Haskell, some are filled with liquid. Balls today also have multiple layers of synthetic materials wrapped around the core. The hardness and softness of a ball's cover material varies: Harder covers help golfers hit balls farther, while softer covers spin more when struck, which allows golfers to spin the ball more so they can stop them where they want them on the green. The number of dimples and the dimple patterns on the surface of balls also vary.

The core, however, is the ball's most important element. Bill Morgan, head of research and development for the Titleist golf ball company, states, "Plain and simple, the core is the engine of the golf ball."[66] His claim is true because of a physics law known as the coefficient of restitution (COR), which refers to how much kinetic energy—energy that provides motion to another object—is transferred in a collision of two objects. A coefficient of 1.0 means that all the energy is transmitted to an object when it is struck. Ball manufacturers try to achieve a COR as close to 1.0 as possible because the more energy that is transferred to the ball, the farther the ball goes—and distance is something every golfer wants. But when a golf club strikes a ball, a fraction of energy is lost because it is converted into heat and more energy escapes through deformation of the ball. At impact a ball is briefly compressed out of its round shape, a phenomenon that can be captured on film. Developing a strong core to prevent deformation is key to achieving a high COR, because it stabilizes the ball's physical structure.

Modern Golf Clubs

Winston Churchill, a British statesman and author who guided England through World War II as prime minister, once jokingly stated, "Golf is a game whose aim is to hit a very small ball into an even smaller hole, with weapons singularly ill-designed for the purpose."[67] For much of golf's long history, that claim was true. The earliest clubs had shafts and heads handcarved from wood. Wood shafts made of hickory were the most popular in the late nineteenth century, because they were flexible and helped players hit balls farther. Blacksmiths made crude irons that were heavy, thick, and difficult to swing until the late 1870s, when modern machines were able to make clubs with greater refinement. New techniques also allowed factories to produce better wood heads.

The earliest clubs were simple in design and function and bear little resemblance to modern-day golf clubs. The rutter, for example, was a long, thin club used solely to knock golf balls out of ruts made by wagon wheels. Club technology improved only slightly for centuries. Around 1902, companies began making steel shafts, which gave golfers more

length and greater consistency when hitting their shots. In 1908 companies began putting grooves on the faces of irons because they imparted more backspin to balls, which helped golfers hit them a longer distance.

It was not until the late twentieth century, however, that manufacturers began using science to create better clubs. One of the most important developments in club technology was the oversize driver, which itself was made possible by the introduction in the 1970s of metal woods—clubs made of metal instead of wood. For most of the twentieth century, driver heads had only measured about 9 cubic inches (149cu cm). But in the 1990s, metal drivers with bigger heads, such as the Big Bertha made by Callaway Golf, became so popular that they made wood drivers and smaller metal drivers extinct. The first Big Bertha was only 11.6 cubic inches (190cu cm) but even that small jump in size helped bad golfers hit more good shots.

Bigger drivers have a small area in the center of the club-face called the "sweet spot." Whenever golfers hit their ball using the sweet spot, they produce great shots. Golfers originally learned that drivers had sweet spots because they could

Big-head drivers like Callaway Golf's Big Bertha club, with their larger "sweet spots" and the force generated by their increased mass, became popular beginning in the 1990s.

HOLE IN ONE

The advantage of a titanium driver is that this metal is lighter than other metals, which allows golfers to swing faster and hit the ball farther.

see that off-center hits were never as good. Physics theories developed in the twentieth century enabled scientists to explain that the sweet spot was the point of maximum potential for transferring energy in the club's collision with the ball. Thus, hitting the sweet spot produces the best shots and is the scientific reason why swings that miss that vital spot do not go as far or as straight. Club manufacturers began making bigger heads, because they could have bigger sweet spots that would help all golfers hit better shots.

Another scientific reason that bigger heads are better can be derived from Newton's second law of motion on how one object reacts when struck by another. The formula to calculate the force of the collision between two bodies depends on the relative mass of both objects. Thus, as the mass of the club increased, so did the force it could impart to the ball. Development of large-headed drivers showed the value of using physics to design clubs, and that success opened up a new era in club manufacturing based on science.

Golf Club Design

In the battle to get golfers to buy their drivers, golf manufacturers kept making them larger and larger until the USGA capped the size of clubheads at 28 cubic inches (460cu cm) in 2004. There had never been any been big-headed wood drivers, because they would have been so heavy that golfers would have not been able to swing them very fast, and swing speed is key to distance in a golf shot. But hollow-headed drivers made of new, lightweight metals, such as titanium, allowed golfers to swing fast even though the heads were bigger. This resulted in longer drives, something every golfer desires.

Club manufacturers also began making clubfaces very thin to increase their COR. Thinner faces deform more at impact than thicker ones, but when the thinner face recovers by returning to its natural shape, it acts like a trampoline, producing a spring-like effect that rockets the ball off the face faster and propels it farther.

A "Simpler and Easier" Game

American professional golfer Jack Nicklaus, who retired in 2005, admits that technological advancements in golfing equipment made it easier for him and other golfers to play better. But Nicklaus, one of the best players in golf history, is worried that technology has changed the game for the worse. He says that equipment improvements have made the game so easy that golfers no longer need to develop as many skills as they once did to play. Nicklaus explains,

> The game in terms of equipment barely changed for 60 years. Then with the equipment revolution that began with metal club heads in the '80s and accelerated with dramatic ball technology in the late '90s, the game changed radically. The best players suddenly found themselves able to hit shots more easily and consistently, as well as pull off shots they never would have tried in the past. It made the game for elite players simpler and easier. So why do I think this is bad for the professional or competitive game? Because modern players don't have to develop the skills they used to and are not as well-rounded as they should be.

Quoted in Jaime Diaz. "I've Been Thinking." *Golf Digest*, March 2007. www.golfdigest.com/magazine/2007-03/diaz_nicklaus.

Club makers also made key improvements in drivers to decrease their moment of inertia (MOI), an object's ability to resist rotating about a given axis, in this case the club's shaft. In a perfect swing the clubface hits the ball squarely with the sweet spot. If the club fails to strike the ball there, then the collision causes the club to rotate left or right around the shaft, and this change in the clubface's angle sends the ball off the intended path. Utilizing physics principles, companies designed clubs that moved more weight to the perimeter of the head because that minimizes MOI and helps golfers hit straighter shots even on mishits. Zumerchik explains, "With the weight of these larger-headed 'hollow' drivers concentrated around the perimeter (in the face, surrounding walls, sole, and crown), the [club maker] is able to adjust the weight locally to increase the momentum transfer potential and to resist twisting from off-center contact away from the sweet spot."[68]

Irons and Putters

The quality of irons also improved greatly in the twentieth century, when factories became capable of mass-producing them to rigid specifications of shape and weight. The heads were created from thin blocks of carbon steel in a process known as forging, which involves heating metal and shaping it manually or with machines. The finished head was then plated with chrome to make it resistant to wear and shiny, which improved its appearance. Today they are known as blade irons, because they are thin compared to modern irons.

In the 1960s several companies began making cast-iron clubs. Casting is a process in which liquid metal is poured into a mold; when the metal cools, it takes on the shape of

Modern irons are made with a cavity in the back that reduces twisting upon impact and improves the accuracy of a shot.

the mold. This process allowed manufacturers greater flexibility in designing irons, including the ability to place hollow spots in clubheads. It also allowed club makers to incorporate principles based on the sweet spot and MOI in designing clubs that made it easier for golfers to hit shots. The result was the cavity-back iron. Unlike flat-backed blades, cavity backs have rounded ridges of thick metal on the head's rear perimeter that leaves a cavity. Cavity-back irons are perimeter weighted to reduce twisting on impact and enable golfers to hit decent shots even if they miss the sweet spot. Irons also became larger to create bigger sweet spots. Golf instructor Mike Southern explains their benefits: "[The changes to irons meant] bad shots were neither as far offline nor suffered as much of a distance penalty as the old blades. In addition, by moving more weight to the sole of the club, cavity backs made it easier to get the ball off the ground. [They worked so well that] 'game improvement clubs' became the most popular name for cavity-back designs."[69]

Putters were once very simple with small narrow heads that looked like flat blades, but new designs inspired by physics principles have radically changed the way putters look. Although putters were the first to incorporate perimeter weighting, the design of the first ones differed only slightly from older putters. But newer designs with perimeter weighting feature odd shapes, such as circular tubes or metal wings extending backward from the putter, with some looking more like branding irons than golf clubs. Designers have also incorporated softer metals in the face that provide a smoother roll when the putter strikes the ball.

In the 1970s the development of graphite shafts made from carbon fiber also boosted the power of golf clubs. The advantage of graphite shafts over steel shafts is that they weigh less—a steel driver shafts weighs between 4 and 4.4 ounces (113gm and 125gm), while a graphite shaft weighs 2.3 to 2.5 ounces (65gm to 71gm). Because graphite shafts weigh less, golfers can generate more swing speed and thus more length. In a *Golf Digest* magazine experiment, a mechanical device using a five-iron with a graphite shaft was able to hit a ball between 4 and 5 yards (3.7m and 4.6m) farther than when it used a metal-shafted five-iron.

Manufacturers today also make graphite shafts that better fit individual golfers by varying their stiffness. How fast golfers swing is what determines the staff stiffness that best suits them. Golfers with swings of more than 100 miles per hour (161kmh) need a stiff or even extrastiff shaft, because their swing is so powerful. Other shafts matched to golfers' swing speeds include those for male golfers with slower swing speeds, and shafts designed for seniors and women, who usually swing more slowly and with less force. Using a shaft that matches their swing speeds helps golfers to more consistently hit the best and longest shots they are capable of hitting.

Significant Changes

New technologies have helped golfers hit balls straighter, but the most significant improvement has been in distance. When the PGA Tour began keeping driving-distance statistics in 1980, American Dan Pohl led with an average drive of 274 yards (251m). In 2012 American Bubba Watson's average drive of 316 yards (289m) led the tour. That overall increase in drive yardage happened despite USGA efforts to limit the size of driver heads and the spring-like effects of driver faces. According to golf experts, improvements in golf balls are the primary reason golfers continue to hit the ball farther than ever.

Although new technology has made golf easier for amateurs and professionals alike, some golfers believe it has hurt the sport. One of them is Nick Price of Zimbabwe, a top-ranked professional golfer in the 1990s. Price believes the increased yardage that technology has produced has negatively affected some of the historic golf courses. Professional golfers are hitting balls so far that St. Andrews Links in Scotland and Augusta National Golf Club in the United States have had to lengthen holes on their courses by creating new tees for professionals, so the courses will not be too easy for them. According to Price, changing the configurations of holes on such courses has destroyed part of their historic significance. He states, "Look what the modern equipment has done to the great old courses. It's made many of them somewhat redundant. To me, that's a sad thing. Other sports haven't had to change their arenas. Golf has."[70]

NOTES

Chapter 1: The History of Golf

1. Arnold Palmer. *My Game and Yours*. New York: Simon & Schuster, 1965, p. 9.
2. George Peper. *The Story of Golf*. New York: TV Books, 1999, p. 17.
3. Quoted in Thomas P. Stewart, ed. *A Tribute to Golf: A Celebration in Art, Photography and Literature*. Harbor Springs, MI: Stewart, Hunter & Associates, 1990, p. 78.
4. Geoff Shackleford. *Grounds for Golf: The History and Fundamentals of Golf Course Design*. New York: Thomas Dunne, 2003, p. 11.
5. Quoted in Robert R. McCord. *Golf: An Album of Its History*. Short Hills, NJ: 1998, p. 25.
6. Quoted in George Peper. *Two Years in St. Andrews: At Home on the 18th Hole*. New York: Simon & Schuster, 2006, p. 85.
7. Quoted in Bob Harig. "Rule Change Will Ban Anchoring." ESPN.com, November 28, 2012. http://espn.go.com/golf/story/_/id/8685514/usga-ra-clear-way-ban-anchoring-putters-2016.
8. Peper. *The Story of Golf*, p. 20.
9. Herbert Warren Wind. *The Story of American Golf*. New York: Callaway Editions, 2000, p. 112.

Chapter 2: Golf and Physics

10. Quoted in Alan Shipnuck. "Power and Grace." *Sports Illustrated*, April 16, 2012. http://sportsillustrated.cnn.com/vault/article/magazine/MAG1197108/index.htm.
11. Quoted in Cameron Morfit. "With a Shot Only He Could Hit, Bubba Watson Wins Masters in Playoff." GOLF.com, April 8, 2012. www.golf.com/tour-and-news/shot-only-he-could-hit-bubba-watson-wins-masters-playoff.
12. John McLester and Peter St. Pierre. *Applied Biomechanics: Concepts and Connections*. Belmont, CA: Wadsworth, 2007, p. 360.
13. Quoted in University of Tennessee. "Newton's Three Laws of Motion." University of Tennessee. http://csep10.phys.utk.edu/astr161/lect/history/newton3laws.html.
14. Theodore P. Jorgensen. *The Physics of Golf*, 2nd ed. New York: Springer-Verlag, 1999, p. 4.

15. John Zumerchik. *Newton on the Tee: A Good Walk Through the Science of Golf*. New York: Simon & Schuster, 2002, p. 14.
16. Greg Norman. "Tip #52: Fades and Draws." Shark.com. www.shark.com/sharkwatch/instruction/tip52.php.
17. Greg Norman. "Tip #19: Learn the Basics of Sand Play." Shark.com. www.shark.com/sharkwatch/instruction/tip19.php.
18. John Wesson. *The Science of Golf*. England: Oxford University Press, 2009, p. 148.
19. Zumerchik. *Newton on the Tee*, p. 98.
20. Zumerchik. *Newton on the Tee*, p. 219.

25. Davies and DiSaia. *Golf Anatomy*, p. 8.
26. Archimedes. "The Lever Quotations." New York University. www.math.nyu.edu/~crorres/Archimedes/Lever/LeverQuotes.html.
27. Zumerchik. *Newton on the Tee*, p. 16.
28. Wesson. *The Science of Golf*, p. 148.
29. Dave Pelz. "Dave Pelz on Pendulum Putting." MeetingsNet, April 1, 1997. http://meetingsnet.com/corporate-meetings/dave-pelz-pendulum-putting.
30. Wesson. *The Science of Golf*, p. 12.
31. Jorgensen. *The Physics of Golf*, p. 52.

Chapter 3: Golf Biomechanics

21. Patria A. Hume, Justin Keogh, and Duncan Reid. "The Role of Biomechanics in Maximising Distance and Accuracy of Golf Shots." *Sports Medicine*, 2005. http://coewww.rutgers.edu/classes/mae/mae473/golf_biomechanics.pdf.
22. Vijay Vad with Dave Allen. *Golf RX: A 15-Minute-a-Day Core Program for More Yards and Less Pain*. New York: Gotham, 2007, p. 13.
23. Craig Davies and Vince DiSaia. *Golf Anatomy*. Champaign, IL: Human Kinetics, 2010, p. 7.
24. Hume, Keogh, and Reid. "The Role of Biomechanics in Maximising Distance and Accuracy of Golf Shots."

Chapter 4: Training and Conditioning

32. Quoted in Jaime Diaz. "A Teacher Speaks Truth to Power." *Golf Digest*, November 2010. www.golfdigest.com/magazine/2010-11/diaz-tiger-foley.
33. Greg Ditrinco. "In the Swing." *Ski*, June/July 2006, p. 50.
34. Karl Morris. "A Lesson in Learning." Golf Today. www.golftoday.co.uk/proshop/features/2011/a_lesson_in_learning.html.
35. Quoted in Stonehill College. "Golf Study Suggests Methods for Effective Learning." Stonehill College, May 27, 2011. http://204.144.14.20/x23959.xml.
36. John J. Ratey. *A User's Guide to the Brain: Perception, Attention, and*

the Four Theaters of the Brain. New York: Vintage, 2002, pp. 178–179.

37. Davies and DiSaia. *Golf Anatomy*, p. 8.

38. Quoted in Roy S. Johnson. "From Cub to Man." *Men's Fitness*, August 2007, p. 102.

39. Davies and DiSaia. *Golf Anatomy*, p. 43.

40. Tiger Woods. "Workout Regimen." TigerWoods.com. http://web.tigerwoods.com/fitness/workoutRegimen.

41. Quoted in Lawrence Donegan. "Woods Savours 'Greatest Triumph' After Epic Duel with Brave Mediate." *Guardian*, June 16, 2008. www.guardian.co.uk/sport/2008/jun/17/usopengolf.tigerwoods.

42. Zumerchik. *Newton on the Tee*, p. 170.

43. Vad with Allen. *Golf RX*, p. 15.

Chapter 5: Golf Psychology

44. Quoted in Thomas Merton. *The Way of Chuang Tzu.* New York: New Directions, 1965, p. 158.

45. Jim Taylor. "Sports: The Power of Emotions." *Psychology Today*, December 1, 2010. www.psychologytoday.com/blog/the-power-prime/201012/sports-the-power-emotions.

46. Quoted in Eric Zweig. *Par for the Course: Golf's Best Quotes & Quips*, Buffalo, NY: Firefly, 2007, p. 35.

47. Neil F. Neimark. "Mind/Body Education Center: The Fight or Flight Response." TheBodySoulConnection.com. www.thebodysoulconnection.com/EducationCenter/fight.html.

48. Bob Rotella with Bob Cullen. *Golf Is Not a Game of Perfect.* New York: Simon & Schuster, 1995, p. 114.

49. Quoted in Gary D'Amato. "Stricker Done Dwelling on Ryder Cup Loss." *Milwaukee Journal Sentinel*, December 19, 2012.

50. Quoted in Charlie Brown. "Sport Psychology Lessons from Bubba Watson." Get Your Head in the Game, April 9, 2012. http://headinthegame.net/2012/04/sport-psychology-lessons-bubba-watson.

51. Tiger Woods. *How I Play Golf.* New York: Warner, 2001, p. 238.

52. Quoted in Anees A. Sheikh. *Imagery in Sports and Physical Performance.* Amityville, NY: Baywood, 1994, p. 23.

53. Zumerchik. *Newton on the Tee*, p. 49.

54. Earl Woods with Pete McDaniel. *Training a Tiger: A Father's Guide to Raising a Winner in Both Golf and Life.* New York: HarperCollins, 1997, p. 23.

55. Quoted in Art Spander. "Tiger Woods in Another Zone." *Telegraph*, March 18, 2008. www.telegraph.co.uk/sport/golf/2294786/Tiger-Woods-in-another-zone.html.

56. Janet A. Young and Michelle D. Pain. "The Zone: Evidence of a Universal Phenomenon for Athletes Across Sports." Athletic Insight, November 1999. www.athleticinsight.com/Vol1Iss3/ZonePDF.pdf.

57. Quoted in Zumerchik. *Newton on the Tee*, p. 58.

58. Quoted in Connell Barrett. "Mental Guru Jim Fannin Trains Three Average Joes to Think like Champs." GOLF.com, December 5, 2012. www.golf.com/instruction/mental-coach-luke-donald-trains-three-amateur-golfers.

59. Sian Beilock. *Choke: What the Secrets of the Brain Reveal About Getting It Right When You Have To*. New York: Free Press, 2011, p. 6.

60. Sian Beilock and Tiffany O'Callaghan. "Why We Screw Up When the Heat Is On." *New Scientist*, July 9, 2011, p. 29.

61. Quoted in Brian Halliday. "Tiger Woods Mental Game." Secret Golf Mind. http://secretgolfmind.com/tiger-woods-mental-game.

Chapter 6: Golf Technology

62. Quoted in Stephen Goodwin. "Heroes for the Ages," *Golf Magazine*, December 1997, p. 49.

63. Quoted in Rick Reilly. "Strokes of Genius." GOLF.com, February 22, 2008. www.golf.com/special-features/strokes-genius.

64. Zumerchik. *Newton on the Tee*, p. 78.

65. Herbert Warren Wind. *The Story of American Golf: Volume One: 1888–1941*. New York: Callaway Editions, 2000, p. 60.

66. Quoted in Titleist. "Getting to the Core of Titleist Golf Balls." Titleist, April 11, 2012. www.titleist.com/teamtitleist/b/tourblog/archive/2012/04/11/getting-to-the-core-of-titleist-golf-balls.aspx.

67. Quoted in Al Barkow, David Barrett, and Ken Janke. *Wit & Wisdom of Golf: Insightful Truths & Bad Lies*. Lincolnwood, IL: Publications International, 1998, p. 33.

68. Zumerchik. *Newton on the Tee*, p. 133.

69. Mike Southern. "Blades vs. Cavity Back Irons." Golfsmith. http://golftips.golfsmith.com/blades-vs-cavity-back-irons-2404.html.

70. Quoted in Tom Callahan. "There Was a Time." *Golf Digest*, February 2013, p. 87.

acceleration: The rate of change in velocity of an object.

aerodynamics: The study of forces acting on objects moving through the air.

air resistance: The force of air pushing against a moving object.

biomechanics: The study of how the body moves and how forces act on the body.

drag: Resistance that airflow causes.

energy: The ability to do work (or to produce change).

flexibility: The ability muscle tissue has to stretch in a range of motion around a joint.

force: Something that pushes or pulls on an object in a certain direction.

friction: A force that resists motion whenever the surfaces of two objects rub against each other.

gravity: The force of attraction between masses.

kinetic energy: Energy possessed by an object due to its motion.

lever: A simple machine consisting of a rigid bar that is free to pivot on a fulcrum.

mass: The amount of matter an object contains.

physics: The study of matter and energy.

proprioception: The brain function that allows people to feel how their body is functioning while performing an action.

simple machine: A machine that requires only the force of a human to perform work.

trajectory: The path of a moving object.

velocity: The rate at which an object changes its position.

work: The transfer of energy resulting from a force acting to move an object over a distance. Work = force x distance.

FOR MORE INFORMATION

Books

Craig Davies and Vince DiSaia. *Golf Anatomy*. Champaign, IL: Human Kinetics, 2010. This book offers a detailed look at biomechanics and includes excellent illustrations of muscles and joints that show how the body works.

Theodore P. Jorgensen. *The Physics of Golf*, 2nd ed. New York: Springer-Verlag, 1999. This book provides a scientific look at the physics involved in golf.

John McLester and Peter St. Pierre. *Applied Biomechanics: Concepts and Connections*. Belmont, CA: Wadsworth, 2007. This book explains the relationship between biomechanics and various sports.

George Peper. *The Story of Golf*. New York: TV Books, 1999. This book is a well-written, interesting history of golf.

George Peper. *Two Years in St. Andrews: At Home on the 18th Hole*. New York: Simon & Schuster, 2006. This is the memoir of golfer, author, scriptwriter, and former *Golf Magazine* editor George Peper about his first two years living in a townhouse overlooking the eighteenth hole of Old Course, a famous golf course at St. Andrews Links in St. Andrews, Scotland.

Vijay Vad with Dave Allen. *Golf RX: A 15-Minute-a-Day Core Program for More Yards and Less Pain*. New York: Gotham, 2007. This book explains how golfers can improve their game through physical fitness.

John Wesson. *The Science of Golf*. England: Oxford University Press, 2009. This is a solid book on how science can help people understand golf.

John Zumerchik. *Newton on the Tee: A Good Walk Through the Science of Golf*. New York: Simon & Schuster, 2002. This book offers various scientific aspects of golf explained in an easy, understandable way.

Internet Sources

Jaime Diaz. "A Teacher Speaks Truth to Power." *Golf Digest*, November 2010. www.golfdigest.com/magazine/2010-11/diaz-tiger-foley. This article is about Sean Foley, a golf instructor who has trained many well-known professional golfers.

GolfClubRevue. "Golf Club History." GolfClubRevue. www.golf-club-revue.com/golf-club-history.html. This is an interesting article about the history and development of golf clubs.

Patria A. Hume, Justin Keogh, and Duncan Reid. "The Role of Biomechanics in Maximising Distance and Accuracy of Golf Shots." *Sports Medicine*, 2005. http://coewww.rutgers .edu/classes/mae/mae473/golf_ biomechanics.pdf. This article has some interesting information on golf biomechanics.

Michael Major. "Ball Flight Law." PGA Michael Major, March 31, 2009. www .majorgolflesson.com/ball-flight-law. This article discusses the science of ball flight.

Karl Morris, "A Lesson in Learning." Golf Today. www.golftoday.co.uk/ proshop/features/2011/a_lesson_in_ learning.html. This article discusses how golfers learn to play golf.

Bob Rotella with Alan Pittman. "10 Rules for How to Win *Your* Major." *GolfDigest*, June 2009. www.golfdigest .com/magazine/2009-06/bobrotella_ 10rules. This article offers good tips on how golfers can control their mind.

Jim Taylor. "Sports: The Power of Emotions." *Psychology Today*, December 1, 2010. www.psychologytoday .com/blog/the-power-prime/201012/ sports-the-power-emotions. This article discusses the emotions golfers must deal with and how to handle them.

University of Tennessee. "Newton's Three Laws of Motion." University of Tennessee. http://csep10.phys .utk.edu/astr161/lect/history/ newton3laws.html. This article provides a good explanation of Sir Isaac Newton's laws of motion.

Periodicals

Sian Beilock and Tiffany O'Callaghan. "Why We Screw Up When the Heat Is On." *New Scientist*, July 9, 2011. This is an interesting interview with University of Chicago psychology professor Sian Beilock, who has researched why athletes choke.

Websites

The Physics of Golf (http://ffden-2 .phys.uaf.edu/211_fall2002.web. dir/josh_fritts). This website offers various articles about the physics of golf.

The Tutelman Site (www.tutelman .com). This website offers some interesting articles on golf physics and other scientific aspects of the sport.

USGA Museum (www.usgamuseum .com). This is the website for the United States Golf Association Museum in Bernards Township, New Jersey. It offers interesting information about the history of golf.

INDEX

A

Addressing the shot, 40–41, *48*
Aerobic training, 61
Aerodynamics, 30–33, *31*
African Americans and golf, 18, 22
Age, 63, 64, *64*
Altitude, 33
Amateur Golf Association, 17
Applied Biomechanics (McLester and St. Pierre), 27
Archimedes, 47
Astronauts, 81
Atmospheric conditions, 33
Augusta National Golf Club, 23, 92

B

Backspin, 30–31, *31*
Backswing, *41*, 42–43, *48*
Ball aerodynamics, 30–33, *31*
Belgium, 9–10
Big Bertha, 87, *87*
Big-head drivers, 87–88
Biomechanics
    address and backswing, 40–43
    applications to golf, 38–39
    downswing, 43–44
    follow-through, 44–47
    lever action of the swing, 47
    putting, 48–50
Body awareness, *56*, 56–57
Body types, 50–51, *51*
Boros, Julius, 63

C

Callaway Golf, 87, *87*
Cast-iron clubs, 90–91
Cavity back irons, 91

Champions Tour, 64
Chicago Golf Club, 20, 21
China, 10, *10*
Choking, 77–78
Chole, 9–10
Chuang-tzu, 65
Churchill, Winston, 86
Clubhouses, 16
Clubs. *See* Golf clubs
Coefficient of restitution, 86, 88
Colonialism, 19–20
Competition, 65
Confidence, 67
Courses. *See* Golf courses

D

Dakyu, 9
Design, golf course, 13–14
Dimples, ball, *82*, 83, 85
Direct learning, 55
Distance of holes, 17–18, 92
Distance of shots, 29–30, 80–81, 83–84, 92
Distractions, blocking, 74–75
Double pendulum swing, 47
Downswing, 43–44, *48*
Draw, 32
Drivers, 81, *87*

E

Eighteen hole standard, 17
Emotions, 65–67, 69
Equipment. *See* Technology

F

Fade, 32–33
Faldo, Nick, 78

Featheries, 82–83
First law of motion, Newton's, 26
"First-tee jitters," 66–67
Fitness, physical, 58–61
Flexibility, 60
Flight-or-fight response, 68–70
Focusing on each shot,
    72–74, 79
Follow through, swing, 44–47, *46*
Force, 27–29
France, 10
Friction and putting, 37

G

Gentlemen Golfers of Leith, 15–16
Golf Anatomy (Davies and DiSaia), 29
Golf balls, *82*, 82–86, *84*
    spin, 30–33
Golf clubs, *87*
    drivers, 81, 86–90
    irons, *90*, 90–91
    launch monitors, 85
    long putters, 19–20
    putters, 91
    shafts, 91–92
Golf courses
    components, *14*
    design,13–14
    hazards, 12–14
    hole distances and technology, 92
    links *vs.* parkland, 12
    private *vs.* public, 21–22
    United States, 20–21
Golf RX (Vad), 62
Grant, George Franklin, 9
Graphite shafts, 91–92
Gravity, 26
Great Britain, 19–20
Ground reaction force, 29
Gutta-percha, 82–83

H

Haskell, Coburn, 84–85
Hazards, 12–14, 33, *34*, 35
History

changes in the game, 8–9, 80–81, 92
    courses, 12–15
    Great Britain, 19–20
    origins of golf, 9–11
    rules, 15–19
    United States, *19*, 20–21
Hooks, 32
Horsepower, 45

I

Injuries, 61–64
Irons, *90*, 90–91

J

James II (king of Scotland), 12
James VI (king of Scotland), 12
Japan, 9
Jeu de mail, 10
Jones, Bobby, 80

K

Kinematic chain, 27, 39–40
Kinetic chain, 44
Kite, Tom, 70–71
Kolven, 10–11

L

Launch monitors, 85
Laws of motion, Newton's. *See* Newton's laws of
    motion
Learning to play, 52–55, *53, 54*
Legends Tour, 64
Levers, 47, 48
Lift, ball, 30–32
Links courses, 12
Long putters, 19–20

M

Magnolia Golf Course, 35
Magnus, Heinrich Gustav, 83
Magnus effect, *82*, 83
Mary (queen of Scotland), 12, *13*
Masters Tournament, 23–24, 72, 80–81
Metal drivers, 87

Mistakes, 70–71
Molecular changes, 27
Moment of inertia, 89–90, 91
Moon landing (1971), 81
Motor learning, 54–55
Muscles, *8*, 27–28, 42, 45–46, 60–61

N

Negative emotions, 67–69
Nelson, Byron, 75
Nervousness, 66–67
Netherlands, 10–11
Neuroscience, 55–57, 74
New York, *19*, 20
Newton's laws of motion, 24–26, *25*, 36–37
    First law of motion, 26
    Second law of motion, 26, 88
    Third law of motion, 26, 29, 83
Nicklaus, Jack, 63, 67, *72*, 74, 80, 89
Norman, Greg, 32, 77–78, *78*

O

Oosthuizen, Louis, 23
Origins of the game, 9–11, *10*
Ouimet, Francis, *21*, 22

P

Paganica, 9
Palmer, Arnold, 9
"Paralysis by analysis," 77
Parkland courses, 12
Pendulum-like swing, 47–50
Perimeter weighting, 91
Physical fitness, 58–61
Physics
    ball aerodynamics, 30–33
    clubhead size, 88
    drivers, 89–90
    golf ball dimples, *82*, 83
    hazard shots, 33, 35
    Newton's laws of motion, 24–26, *25*, 29, 36–37,
        83, 88
    the swing, 26–30
The Physics of Golf (Jorgensen), 45
Pohl, Dan, 92

Popularity, 9, 22
Power, 42, 45
Preshot routines, *72*, 72–73
Preston, Robert Adams, 83
Price, Nick, 92
Private clubs, 21–22
Professional Golf Association, 18
Proprioception, 56–57
Psychology
    choking, 77–78
    distractions, blocking, 74–75
    emotions, 65–67
    focusing on each shot, 72–74
    sports psychology, 73
    stress of the game, 67–71, *68*
    the zone, being in, 75–77
Public courses, 22
Putters, 19–20, 91
Putting, *36, 49*
    biomechanics, 48–50
    Newton's laws of motion, 36–37

R

Race/ethnicity, 18
Ray, Ted, 22
Reid, John, *19*, 20
Revolutions per minute, 31
Rome, ancient, 9
Rotella, Bob, 70–71, *71*
Rough, hitting from the, 35
Royal and Ancient Golf Club of St. Andrews, *15*, 17
Rules and standards, 15–19, 85, 88
Running, *58*, 61
Rush, Benjamin, 11

S

Sand traps, 33, *34*, 35
The Science of Golf (Wesson), 42
Scotland
    Gentlemen Golfers of Leith, 15–16
    origins of golf, 9, 11–12
    Royal and Ancient Golf Club of St. Andrews, 17
Second law of motion, Newton's, 88
"Selective amnesia," 71
Seniors, 64, *64*
Shafts, 91–92

Shepard, Alan, 81, *81*
Sidespin, 32
Sifford, Charlie, 18, *18*
Slices, 32
Snead, Sam, 18
Socioeconomic class, 21, 22
Spin, ball, 30–33
Sports Medicine (Hume, Keogh, and Reid), 39
Sports psychology, 73
St. Andrew's Golf Club, Yonkers, NY, *19,* 20
St. Andrews Links, *15*
    as birthplace of golf, 8
    hazards, 33
    hole distances, 92
    rules, evolution of, 17
    seaside location, 12
Straight hitting, 30
Stress of the game, 67–71, *68*
Stretching, 60, 63–64
Stricker, Steve, 71
Suigan, 10, *10*
Sweet spots, 87–88, 91
Swing
    accuracy, 50
    address, 40–41
    backswing, 42–43
    body mechanics, *42*
    body rotation, *41*
    body types, 50–51, *51*
    double pendulum swing, *48*
    follow through, 44–47, *46*
    force of, 27–29
    golf club design, 92
    injuries, *61*, 62–63
    kinematic chain, 39–40
    muscle involvement, *28*
    physics, 26–30, *40*
    putting, 47–50, *49*
    sand traps, 34, 35
    speed of, 29
    two-lever action, 47

T

Tait, Peter Guthrie, 32
Taylor, William, 83
Teaching methods, 52–55, *54*

Technology
    changes in the game, 8–9
    golf balls, *82,* 82–86, *84*
    golf clubs, 19–20, 81, 86–92, *87, 90*
Terminology, 16
Third law of motion, Newton's, 29, 83
Titanium drivers, 88
Training, *58,* 58–61

U

United States, history of golf in the, 17, *19,* 20–21
United States Golf Association, 17, 85, 88
U.S. Open, 22, 61–62

V

Vad, Vijay, 62
Vardon, Harry, 22
Video as a teaching tool, 53–54, *54*
Visualization, 73–74

W

Watson, Bubba, 23–24, 72, 92
Weather, 33
Weight lifting, 60–61
Whistling Straits course, 33
Wind, 33
Women, 22
Woods, Earl, 52, 75
Woods, Tiger, *58, 75*
    African Americans and golf, 18
    concentration, 79
    distance of shots, 80–81
    distractions, blocking, 75
    "first-tee jitters," 67
    injuries, 61–63
    learning to play golf, 52
    preshot routine, 72–73
    training, 58–61
    the zone, being in, 75–76
Working memory, 77

Z

Zone, being in the, 75–76

PICTURE CREDITS

ABOUT THE AUTHOR

Michael V. Uschan is the author of more than ninety books, including *Life of an American Soldier in Iraq* for Lucent Books, for which he won the 2005 Council for Wisconsin Writers Juvenile Nonfiction Award. It was the second time he won the award. He began his career as a writer and editor with United Press International, a wire service that provided stories to newspapers, radio, and television. Uschan considers writing books a natural extension of the skills he developed in his many years as a journalist. He and his wife, Barbara, reside in the Milwaukee suburb of Franklin, Wisconsin.